As a way of saying thanks for your purchase, I'm offering you free downloads and audio interviews that's exclusive to my readers.

Building a referral based business with agents requires a certain mindset and skills. That's why I wrote: Instant Referrals for Mortgage Professionals.

You'll hear interview with top producing Mortgage Professionals who are succeeding in building profitable real estate agents referrals - with less stress and hassle than most.

You Can Download Your Free Gifts Here:
http://www.GetInstantReferrals.com

What Mortgage Professionals Are Saying

"Instant Referrals™ delivered results for my team. We captured 87 agents, got referrals and deals! If you want to quickly and easily capture agents, Instant Referrals™ is your ticket in today's market."

Sue Woodard President
President
Vantage Production

"I wanted to express my appreciation for sharing your expertise in this area. You clearly outlined the steps, ideas, and follow up strategies that loan officers can utilize immediately to increase Realtor partnerships and referrals. Well done!"

Dustin Hughes
Owner/Mortgage Advisor
Northwest Mortgage Advisors

"We Set Meetings With 19 Agents Within A Few Days of The Seminar!" We had 170 registrants and 84 who showed up. Of those roughly 46 agents checked the please contact me box on the survey form. My partner Tom has been following up and so far has 19 appointments, one of them with a "Top 20" agent who has 115 listings and funds more than $20 million annually. All the agents loved it and can't wait for the next one.

Paul Dunn
Sunstreet Mortgage
Tucson, AZ

What Mortgage Professionals Are Saying

"Implementing just one idea from Instant Referrals™ exploded my agent seminars from 10-15 agents to over 80 agents at each seminar!

Brian Kludt
Senior Mortgage Planner/Branch Manager
Waterstone Mortgage

"I Have No Doubt The Seminar Was Worth My Time and Money. I'll Be Quite Busy Setting Appointments. Our market only has about 500 agents, and we had 80 sign up with 67 actually attending. An 83% show rate! The best part for me is that most agents took the time to fill out the survey. Many indicated they had issues with their current lender. I will be quite busy for the next 30 days following-up and it will be so much easier asking for appointments because of the survey form!"

Darla Watts
Loan Officer Sterling
Savings Bank

"Our Seminar Was Fantastic! It Was Rated Excellent By 98% Of The Agents Attending. I Would Recommend This To Anyone Looking To Increase Their Business. It worked! I would wholeheartedly recommend this type of marketing to anyone looking to increase their business."

Bonnie Oliver
Sales Manager
Guraranty Mortgage
Onalaska, WI

What Mortgage Professionals Are Saying

"Your System is the absolute best use of time and resources for contacting agents! We had 146 reservations and 105 agents who attended. I would recommend any mortgage broker NOT in my area book your event before someone else does. We're looking forward to our next one with you!"

Bob Garrity
Branch Manager
Preferred Mortgage
San Rafael, CA

"Almost 200 Agents attended, many of whom are current clients and many new prospects who we're following up with and getting good activity from. Instant Referrals™ is the quickest, most effective way to get in front of LOTS of agents fast and build your pipeline."

Blaine Brunson
Assistant Vice President/Sales
Fidelity National Title
Scottsdale, AZ

"Your seminar system is a game changer. With just one event I captured five new agents who sent me and I got invited to host monthly training sessions for agents of a large local Century 21 who already have an in-house lender. That from just one event – amazing!"

Michael Citron
CEO Dispute Suite
Tampa, FL

What Mortgage Professionals Are Saying

"We just completed our first Instant Referrals™ Seminar and I am very pleased with how it went. As far as the mechanics of holding the seminar you made it very easy to pull the seminar together. All of the details have been thought of and you actually took care of many of them. For those of us who are not experienced at holding seminars, this was invaluable. It was a very efficient and easy way to meet a whole group of agents at one time!"

Cheryl Sheasby
Mortgage Network Solutions
Warren, NJ

"Thanks for including me among your elite group of Seminar Speakers. One thing I am always striving for is to arrive at a speaking engagement with a room full of people eager to hear what I have to say. Your Instant Referrals™ Seminar System has virtually guaranteed I'll not only have the full room, but that my hosts and co-sponsors will be equally delighted with the results they get from the event as well as the attendees. It's a true win-win for all parties involved and a tremendous value-add for those mortgage professionals looking to grow their agent referrals."

Ed Lyon
President, Tax Coach

What Mortgage Professionals Are Saying

"Your Instant Referrals™ seminar system has proven to be the absolute best method for getting LOT's of agents out to attend my events. I speak to agents all across the world and the events that you put on are by far the most. You have "cracked to code" for any loan officer looking to quickly build agent referrals. I just about require any mortgage company booking me for a speaking engagement to use your system for maximum results!"

Walter Sanford
President
Sanford Systems

"We secured 15 agent meetings, three new referral partners and $990,000 in originations within 30 days! These are top producers who would normally brush me off and never return my calls. We could not have gotten those results so quickly without your seminar system."

Lee Williams
Loan Consultant
ARC Funding
San Francisco, CA

Instant Referrals for Mortgage Professionals

A Proven System for Capturing More Agents, Closing More Loans and Becoming THE "Go-To" Lender In Your Area

Geoff Zimpfer

Disclaimer

We make every effort to ensure that we accurately represent these products and services and their potential for income. Earning and/or income statements made by our company and/or Independent Representatives are estimates of what you can possibly earn. There is no guarantee that you will make these levels of income and you accept the risk that the earnings and income statements differ by individual. The examples are not to be interpreted as any guarantee, promise, representation and/or assurance. We do not purport our business and/or us as being a 'get rich scheme'.

As with any business, your results may vary, and will be based on your individual capacity, business experience, expertise, and level of desire. There are no guarantees, promises, representations and/or assurances concerning the level of success you may experience. Your level of success in attaining the results claimed depends on the time you devote to the business, the ideas and techniques mentioned, your finances, knowledge and various skills, since such skills and factors differ according to individuals. Testimonials and examples used are exceptional results, which do not, or may not, apply to the average person, and are not intended to guarantee, promise, represent and/or assure that anyone will achieve the same or similar results. We reiterate that each individual's success depends on his or her background, dedication, desire and motivation.

There is no assurance that examples of past earnings can be duplicated in the future. We cannot guarantee your future results and/or success. There are some unknown risks in business and on the Internet that we cannot foresee which can reduce results. We are not responsible for your actions. Any claims made of actual earnings or examples of actual results can be verified upon request.

The use of our information, products and/or services should be based on your own due diligence, which you undertake and confirm that you have carried out to your entire satisfaction. You agree that our company is not liable for any success or failure of your business, acts and/or conduct that is directly or indirectly related to the business and/or the purchase and use of our information, products and/or services.

While all attempts have been made to verify information provided in this book and its associated ancillary arterials, neither the Authors nor the Publisher assumes any responsibility for errors, inaccuracies, or omissions. Any slights of people or organizations are unintentional. If advice concerning legal or related matters is needed, the services of a qualified professional should be sought. This book and/or its associated ancillary materials is not intended for use as a source of legal or accounting advice. Also, some suggestions made in this book and/or its ancillary materials concerning marketing, sales, affiliate relationships and/or referral fees, etc., may have inadvertently introduced practices deemed unlawful in certain states and municipalities. You should be aware of the various laws governing business transactions or other business practices in your particular geographic location.

Any reference to any persons or businesses, whether living or dead, existing or defunct, is purely coincidental.

Also by Geoff Zimpfer:

Speed Marketing for Loan Officers

The New Rules of Real Estate Sales & Marketing

TopAgent TV

The Originator Hot Seat Interview Series

Visit The Blog

www.LoanOfficerMarketingTV.com

Table of Contents

Acknowledgements

A special thank you to my fellow Mortgage Professionals who have survived and thrived during these turbulent market challenges, governmental regulations and attack on our personal livelihood – only to rise above it and succeed – you are an inspiration and true professionals!.

Special acknowledgement to Todd Duncan for being among the first in our industry to provide much needed leadership and character that inspired me to keep getting better, especially when times are tough. Tim Braheem, your vision and insights helped me tap into my best. Thanks for raising the bar for us all. Dave Savage, thanks for helping all Mortgage Professionals to understand the importance of education, positioning and giving us the platform to make that possible. Barry Habib; you've got style, grace and you took my call when you didn't have to. Thank you. Sue Woodard, you believed in me even when the bridge collapsed! Thanks for your trust.

Introduction

Who Is Geoff Zimpfer and
Why Should You Listen To Me?

Congratulations!

You're reading this book because you are among the few who "do" as opposed to the many who "talk." You're about to learn a proven, field tested method used by hundreds of Mortgage Originators for finding, capturing and converting REALTORS® into profitable referral partners for your mortgage business. You'll also discover how you can finally eliminate the common frustrations most originators struggle with when trying to get business from REALTORS®.

Just imagine, no more cold-calling, no more weenie-head agents, no more struggling to reach top producers and get agent loyalty. No more agents saying; "I just give my buyers three lender cards and they choose." Please!

What Tony Robbins Told Me
One Evening Over Dinner

I know it's possible because just nine years ago, at the age of 37, I was at a crossroads. I had spent ten years mostly as a promoter and Field Sales Trainer for Anthony Robbins, America's #1 Agent Walter Sanford, Real Estate Marketing firm Hobbs & Herder and other well-known authors, speakers and "success" authorities.

With Tony Robbins circa 1990

During my those ten years traveling the globe, I had the good fortune to spend a lot of time working with REALTORS®, Mortgage Originators and many other high achieving professionals. I say good fortune because that experience and insight became very useful at a pivotal moment in my career – which I'll share with you in just a moment.

I remember one evening, our team having dinner with Tony, as we regularly did, every six weeks. We just wrapped up our seminar where over those six weeks; we gave hundreds of presentations, seminars and mini-workshops to thousands of salespeople in local companies resulting in over 2,000 people attending Tony's seminar. At dinner that night, I asked him how he became so good at public speaking in such a short period of time.

Tony shared his strategy for becoming a great speaker and persuader in as little time as possible.

Want to know what he said?

His strategy was to simply get in front of more people, more often, than any other speaker. He told us that in his early days, he would speak for free, for food, as many as three times per day, seven days a week to an audience of one or an audience of 100.

His level of commitment allowed him to work on his craft, hone his skills, get feedback and, most importantly, shortcut his outcome; which was to master his speaking and influence skills, reaching thousands and ultimately millions of people worldwide.

Today of course Tony no longer needs to speak for free and is sought out by people of all levels of success from celebrities, to presidents, world leaders and corporate executives.

I know what you're saying..."great story Geoff but what does this have to do with getting more deals from agents?"

Answer: Everything!

Allow me to explain. Just after my first son Zack was born, it hit me like a ton of bricks. I was waiting to catch a flight to Ontario, Canada to give a marketing workshop for a bunch of REALTORS® when all of a sudden a huge knot curled in the pit of my stomach.

I was sick and tired of flying from Seattle to Schenectady and everywhere in between just to earn a living. I missed my family and couldn't see myself doing this for another ten years, let alone another ten days.

I returned from my trip knowing I had to make a career choice: become a REALTOR® or become a Loan Officer? For me, the choice was obvious. I figured after delivering hundreds of sales training workshops to thousands of agents across North America, surely capturing and converting agents to send me loan referrals would be a walk in the park!

Boy was I wrong!

For the first year, I did what most Mortgage Loan Officers do. It seemed pretty simple: If you want to succeed, you have to find buyers. And the way to find them is to hunt down agents by prospecting them.

Everything I observed, everything I heard, and everything I read could be summarized by the following: 'make cold calls, hit open houses, attend Broker Previews, give presentations, run ads, network and so on.

As the end of my first year was approaching, I felt misled, bamboozled, frazzled, and frantic about how I was ever going to get a steady stream of buyers referred to me by my local REALTORS®. What was even more stressful was that because the deals were only trickling in, I had to take a HELOC out on my home to cover my ever-increasing bills during that first year.

With a newborn baby, a stay at home wife, bills piling-up and a growing mortgage to pay, I absolutely had to figure out a way to get purchase loans in my pipeline and fast. I didn't have thousands to spend on advertising. I tried buying leads with little success. I cold-called for agent meetings; I did open houses, hosted happy hours… I did it all.

To be fair, some of those activities did work, but only occasionally. The return on the effort was unpredictable, at best. Besides that, every other loan officer in my city was pretty much doing the same *exact* things I was doing.

I finally realized that doing *more* of what I was doing or even doing what I was doing *better* was not going to make me happy. I wanted to work smart, while working hard to build my business. I wanted more peace of mind, not more pressure. I didn't want to wait two years or even twelve months to start seeing a significant return on my efforts, either. I needed to make money and make it *fast*.

The question I kept asking was:

"How do I quickly get in front of a LOT of REALTORS® fast and convert a good percentage of them into referral partners?"

Have you ever heard it said that your brain is like a computer? Ask it a question and it will give you an answer. Ask it a 'good' question and you'll get an even better answer. Makes sense right?

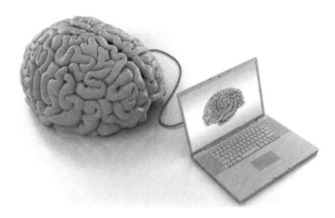

Finally, after repeatedly asking the answer did arrive! I remembered that dinner conversation with Tony Robbins and I had experienced an… *"A-Ha! Moment"*

My *"A-Ha! Moment"* was that I was not following a successful model for quickly finding, capturing and converting agents to referral partners. I was doing what every other loan officer in my office was doing – and they were getting dismal results too!

I woke-up from my coma and decided that I would *break free* from those unproductive activities and do something that appeared to be completely radical. I would host my very own "Wow" factor seminar for Real Estate Agents!

I was overwhelmed with feelings of excitement, joy, exuberance and yes, a slight dose of uncertainty but like Billionaire Sir Richard Branson is fond of saying: "Screw It Let's Do It." I was going to make it happen – no matter what.

SPEED TIP

Whenever you're deciding to get out of your comfort zone, doing something that is deemed by others as crazy or silly or they say "it won't work"; it's helpful to carry a bit of bravado long the way to get you going.

Within this book, you'll discover a 'System' that is hands-down the best way to eliminate the common frustrations of working with REALTORS®, including:

- How to Break Into Closed Offices

- Reaching Top Producers

- Cold Calling Agents (Ugh!)

- Quickly Boosting Your Purchase Referrals

- Eliminating Your Competition
  (Even the in-house Lender!)

- Finally Getting Agent Loyalty

- Creating a Predictable Stream of Purchase Referrals

And more…

The Seminar 'System' works so well I decided to give it an official name: *Instant Referrals*™ **for Mortgage Loan Officers**. It's simple, and easily modeled by any Mortgage Professional – anywhere! The 'System' took me from $0 to $27 Million within just two years and to $37 Million by my third year of originating loans. That may not qualify me as 'superstar originator' but it would put me among the Top 500 Originators in the U.S.!

**How would you like to add $10 Million
in annual fundings to your bottom line in
the next twelve months ~ or less?**

Even better, close to 70% of the loans are purchase business, brought to me on a silver platter by agents with little or no "selling" the buyers on why to use me versus the competition. And I do it with less stress, strain, struggle, and frustration than any Loan Officer I know who chooses to work with agents.

Hosting educational seminars for your local agents will catapult you to achieve not only a high income, but also extraordinary prestige, even celebrity status, among your local agent community; creating a "perpetual motion, purchase money, referral machine" that brings you all of your purchase clients with ABSOLUTELY NO PROSPECTING … and that makes doing loans fun!

After hundreds of inquires from fellow Mortgage Loan Officers seeking more information about how to use this same system for their own business, I finally decided to write the first ever – industry book; sharing with you my own experiences and success stories from fellow Originators across the United States. Our goal is to inspire you to action – so that you too can have the success you deserve in working with agents and start having fun doing loans again!

Instant Referrals™ **is not theory.** It's extremely well thought out and executed repeatedly all across the country in every market, with Mortgage Brokers, Mortgage Bankers, Correspondent Lenders, small firms, big banks, and all others.

My hope for you is that you not only enjoy reading this book, you apply the strategies and tactics revealed to achieve your goals as a Mortgage Professional. We need more professionals in our industry! I look forward to connecting with you – soon.

Let's Get Started!

Geoff Zimpfer

PART ONE

The Fundamentals Never Change

You already know that getting in front of agents and getting referrals is fundamental to your success. The first part of this book introduces you and explains the process for quickly boosting your agent partners and referrals using educational seminars. While maybe not new and sexy, agent seminars are proven, fundamental and the most effective way of creating high value, productive relationships with agents *fast*.

*"The tragedy of life is not that it ends so soon,
but that we wait so long to begin it."*

– Anonymous

Chapter I

Fishing For Agents

Too many Mortgage Professionals struggle to achieve any real, meaningful, long-term success working with agents. Usually it's because they are doing what I was doing – modeling an ineffective system for finding, capturing and converting agents into profitable referral partners.

The Right Bait

Years ago, my family built a beautiful house in Maine on a serene pond with a dock and small boat just a few yards from the house. During the summer, my friends and I would drive up from Boston to visit and enjoy taking the boat out on fishing excursions.

We enjoyed just getting out and cruising along the calm, glass-like water as much as we did spending quality time together, enjoying some laughs trying to get the fish interested in our bait. None of us were skilled anglers by any stretch of your imagination. Fishing as you know is just an excuse to have some beers with your buddies and get away from it all right?

One day we were out of our usual bait – worms – and took a drive down to the local bait shop to get a fresh supply of night crawlers. *That's what they call big fat worms in Maine for you city folk.*

They're called night crawlers because they usually only come out at night. They're about the size of a real small garden snake and everyone says it's what you need if you want to catch fish. They're so popular that catching and making money from selling night crawlers is an entire cottage industry in Maine.

We grabbed our usual Styrofoam container of worms from the refrigerated cooler and set it on the counter when Vern, the old salty guy behind the counter says:

"You boys wanna really catch some fish?"

Vern resembled that character Mr. Quint, the squinty-eyed shark hunter from the movie Jaws.

Well, yeah sure! That's why we're buying these night crawlers. Vern says:

"Might catch a few with them worms but if you want a feedin' frenzy, oughta try some Hellgrammites."

Of course we had no idea what the heck Hellgrammites were but we were very interested in a feeding frenzy of fish – that sounded a lot more exciting than our normal routine of casting our line and waiting for the occasional fish to nibble at our worms.

Hellgrammites? What are they?

Vern says: *"They're baby Dobson flies. Some folks call 'em toe biters cause they have pincers that bite. Best bait you'll ever use. Fish go nuts over 'em. You'll catch more fish in one hour than you would all summer with plain 'ol worms."*

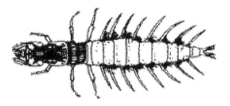

Hellgrammites

That's all we needed to hear from good 'ol Vern. He knew what he was talking about. He'd owned that bait shop for years and was a no B.S. guy who had a way of delivering the truth, not caring much about offending anyone – especially tourists. We bought a box of those Hellgrammites and hurried back to test out our new found secret weapon!

Holy fish frenzy!

Vern wasn't kidding. Each time we put these little buggers on the hook they were aggressively biting away at our fingers. It was all worth it though because they worked exactly like Vern said. We cast our line to our favorite spot and BOOM the fish went crazy! It looked like a school of piranhas were attacking.

We landed at least fifteen fish that day. It was exhilarating! Never before had we caught so many fish so fast and we all agreed, from now on, we're fishing with Hellgrammites!

The Lesson

So what kind of bait are you using to attract and capture Real Estate Agents? "We have great rates and service?" "We're always available 24/7?" "We have quick turnaround times?" "We're professional?" "We really care?"

If you're goal is to land a lot of agents, good agents, your 'bait' has to attract more attention, offer something of value that agents need, want and don't get very often. You want to create your own local "feeding frenzy" that has you landing lots of agents.

Make sense?

Some agents will instantly be keepers and some you may choose to throw back. Others with the proper care and feeding will mature and grow into winners over time. But first you have to get them interested in your offer before they 'bite' so can you hook 'em.

Your bait in today's new economy comes down to a simple formula.

$$E + CV \div R = LR$$
Engagement + Consistent Value ÷ Relationship = Loan Referrals!

How would you like to get more loyalty and consistent referrals from your agents? Your answer is found in applying the formula above.

How do you add consistent value? There's many ways to add value to an agents business and life.

Start by just asking your agents:

"What areas of your business are most important for you right now and why?"

It's a simple question but how an agent answers it can reveal a tremendous amount for you. It can reveal what areas of their business are working and with further questioning, reveal what areas they may be struggling.

Most agents admittedly struggle with common issues in their business. Even top producing agents share the same shortcomings. These areas include:

- Business Planning

- Database Management

- Lead/Client Follow-Up

- Sales / Marketing

- Lead Conversion

- Technology

- Time Management

- Personal Accountability

- Social Media

Your fist objective is to discover what area of the agents business is most important right now – and why – and what personal goals are most important to them both short and long term – and why?

When you become a source of valuable information that improves an agent's business and their life, you are becoming an indispensable asset and resource worthy of attracting top agents and getting referrals versus just another person to get a loan from with some good rates and cool calendars, pens, and notepads to give away.

 As Vern would say: *"Use the right bait you'll have a feedin' frenzy."*

The Right Pond

We learned from Vern the importance of using the right bait for creating a feeding frenzy. Before we left his bait shop that day, Vern also reminded us of another important lesson when you're trying to catch fish.

Vern Says: *"If you want to catch some fish, go where the fish are."*

Simple but true right?

Are you fishing for agents where the agents are?

Where can you consistently find GOOD agents in your local area? The donut shop! (Just kidding. We know who hangs out there☺)

Here's a short checklist for you.

√ **Board Of REALTORS®**

√ **Real Estate Offices (Really?)**

√ **Title/Escrow/Home Warranty Reps**

√ **Broker Previews/Caravan Tours**

√ **Industry Seminars/Trade Shows**

√ **Industry Events/Charity Functions**

√ **Open Houses (Sometimes)**

√ **Local Home for Sale Magazines**

√ Sunday Newspaper Real Estate Section

√ Local Cable TV Channel (Real Estate Shows)

Are You In The Game?

The real question is "how many agents know who *you* are?" If you're not on the field, "in the game" every week, in front of agents, making connections, participating in your local real estate market by engaging where the agents are, building name recognition and awareness – you don't exist.

Many experts – like Tony Robbins, talk about leverage. Using leverage to get more results with less time, energy, money, and effort is the key. Later we'll take a look at how to host your own seminars and classes for agents so you can leverage your time, *fast-track* your results and build your own pond – where the fish (agents) come to YOU!

But first let's take a look at the next critical step in successfully fishing for agents…

The Right Mindset

Perhaps one of the most time-consuming and frustrating activities that Mortgage Professionals engage in is trying to meet with REALTORS® one-on-one, with the intent to build rapport, win their trust, and get a commitment for referrals.

Certainly in the purchase market, REALTORS® are a high-leverage source for getting high-quality, pre-sold, pre-tenderized referrals coming in the door to fill your pipeline with lots of closed deals. You already know it's "live and die by the refi" for those who rely on low rates, especially these days with home equity having vanished in many areas and qualifying for a refinance becoming increasingly more difficult than a purchase loan.

Let me put it to you bluntly;

If you're an originator today and you expect to not just survive but to *thrive* during this transitional market and beyond, a large part of your success will result from how effective you are at generating, capturing, and growing your REALTOR® referred *purchase* business.

If you have any negative baggage attached to working with agents – let it go. If you're not the type who enjoys rolling up your sleeves, teaming-up with agents, and taking a genuine interest in building mutually beneficial relationships – give this book to a colleague who is because that is the currency of success in this New Economy.

What Do Agents Want From You?

After conducting hundreds of interviews with agents at all levels of achievement, we've found that agents want a few simple things from their Mortgage Professional.

1) Timely returned calls and updates regarding files in process.

2) Be truthful and upfront concerning borrowers, underwriting, qualifying, conditions and closing times.

3) Help me with my most important, current business challenges and achieve my goals.

The first two can be done by any Loan Officer – and is the minimum in today's market – although not all Loan Officers do it. You become a Trusted Advisor and team member, building loyalty and longevity from your agents doing all three, consistently and passionately – over time. Not just occasionally or when you feel like it – always. That's the mindset required for success with agents today.

Some of my best friends are agents that began as referral partners. Most are just that – business partners of mutual respect and trust. In today's market, it's reassuring to know I have a referral team as genuinely vested in my success as I am in theirs.

Does that sound attractive to you? Imagine never wondering where your next deal is coming from. Imagine warm calls with buyers referred to you by their trusted agent. What a great way to do business!

Are you ready for it?

*"It is less important to redistribute wealth
than it is to redistribute opportunity."*

– Arthur H. Vandenberg

Chapter 2

Digging for Oil

The 2011 National Association of REALTORS® Profile of Home Buyers and Sellers reveals that even with access to an abundance of information online, consumers still value the services offered by a full-service agents and brokers. The study revealed that home-buyers use a wide variety of resources in searching for a home: 88 percent surf the Internet, **91 percent of buyers who used the Internet to research homes purchased their home through a real estate agent!** The study also revealed that 56 of buyers who used the Internet also used yard signs, 46 percent attend open houses and 30 percent look at print or newspaper ads. Although buyers also use other resources, they generally start the search process online and then contact an agent.

When asked where they first learned about the home purchased, 38 percent of buyers said the Internet; 37 percent of buyers from a real estate agent; 11 percent a yard sign or open house; 6 percent from a friend, neighbor or relative; 4 percent home builders; 2 percent a print or newspaper ad; 2 percent directly from the seller; and less than 1 percent from a home book or magazine.

Here's the key: **Ninety one percent** of home buyers who used the Internet to search for a home purchased through *a real estate agent* – a share that has steadily increased from 69 percent in 2001. Furthermore, real estate agents were viewed as a useful information source by ninety eight percent of buyers who used an agent while searching for a home.

What Does This Mean?

Overwhelmingly, the primary contact point, the top of the funnel and main source of buyers is still your local agent. As the study notes, the trend has been growing not declining.

What about the Internet?

Even though home shopping on their own has never been easier, buyers are still looking to the agent to help them find the right home and a professional agent to help them through the process. Agents who present themselves as honest, caring, knowledgeable, and full-service stand a better chance of engaging buyers.

Even though the market has changed and technology has changed, consumers' expectations remain consistent. Sellers still want their home priced well and marketed well believing that means a faster, more profitable sale and buyers are still looking for a professional agent to guide them through the entire process – including financing their purchase.

Top agents have always known this and they make sure they promote these qualities to both buyers and sellers. That's why they continue to win the business and confidence of consumers. Combine that and the trend towards consumers preference for one-stop shop when it comes to buying a home – what you have here is an oil well!

What's an 'oil well' in your business? An oil well is any source of business that once located, drilled and tapped, continues to produce business. If your business plan includes growing your purchase business so you no longer "live and die by the refi" there simply is no better oil well for originators than our friendly local Real Estate Agent.

You - An Oil Tycoon!

How would you like to own six, seven or even ten oil wells that consistently spew rivers of 'black gold' from the ground and all you have to do is hold your bucket out to catch enough oil and you'll be richer than 'ol Jed Clampett himself?

Just imagine: you could follow in the footsteps of the Beverly Hillbillies and "move to the land of swimming pools and movie stars!"

If you're reading this and don't remember the Beverly Hillbillies – I've just aged myself! You can Google them.

Imagine getting control of your business and financial life. After the last few years, who in this business wouldn't love to have more predictability in their income? Who in this business hasn't dreamt about falling asleep at night no longer worrying about what tomorrow will bring, whether any referrals will come down the pipe to you, or what the current administration is conjuring up to 'fix' the mortgage and real estate market?

Out With The Old

The first thing you're going to have to do in order to build your oil wells and have success beyond your wildest imagination is to strip away some of the old way of thinking, the inefficient methods by which you have done things before.

You will need to change the way you market to, qualify, and meet with real estate agents, the quality of the agents *you* choose as referral partners, and the opportunities you have to get off the wheel of insanity.

How fast would you boost your agent referrals if you were meeting with, let's say, twenty agents at one time? Better yet, how *long* would it take you to get meetings with twenty agents by the usual methods of cold-calling, open houses etc?

Have you ever met one-on-one with twenty agents in your career? Welcome to a whole new way of life and success, building your Real Estate Agent referrals! Now let's go get some oil wells!

Finding Your Oil Wells…Fast!

Most of the frustrations that occur prospecting for agents comes from not having a proven 'system' for finding, drilling, and tapping those agents who will become referral producing 'oil wells' later in time.

Too many of us think in terms of the immediate, the here and now because we are concerned about our earnings … *now*. Not tomorrow or next week. Heck, we're certainly not thinking about these things a year or more into the future.

But if you're going to drill for oil, wouldn't it make sense to have a plan? You wouldn't expect *successful* oil companies to simply drill into the ground out of blind faith, would you?

The first thing you have to do is **find the oil!** Of course we're talking about finding Real Estate Agents – right?

So how do you currently find, market to and attract producing agents right now? For the average Mortgage Loan Officer, that means attending open houses, dropping by offices without invitation, stalking agents on Facebook, cold-calling, running "me-too" marketing campaigns going for "spray and pray" hoping they get lucky and stumble across a few agents, hoping they randomly send the occasional referral our way. That's about as effective as drilling for oil by being blindfolded and throwing darts at a map.

How Most Loan Officers Approach Working With Agents

That's the 'old way' of getting business from agents and it is *completely random*, produces unpredictable or little results that often leads to burnout and frustration. Most originators keep repeating this insanity 'hoping' that they'll hit pay dirt.

Einstein (yeah, pretty smart guy) once said, "Insanity is the act of doing something the same way over and over again and expecting a different result."

If this sounds like you, then eventually you fall prey to the belief that there's no oil in your backyard and you go back to just doing refi's, buying leads, or even cold-calling. Please, don't go back there!

There *is* a better way! I promise you.

Maybe you've hosted seminars for agents and been less than thrilled with your results. I get it. That doesn't mean that seminars don't work, because they do – if you have a *system* that ensures a successful outcome.

If you haven't hosted seminars for agents yet, don't worry. You don't have to be a great speaker or as entertaining as Elvis returned from the grave. When you use the strategies and tips I'll share with you in this book, you'll soon become an oil tycoon, drilling those agent oil wells and earning all the referrals and recognition that come with it.

What is Instant Referrals™ for Mortgage Loan Officers?

At its most basic, *Instant Referrals*™ is a Seminar System or a blueprint for quickly becoming the premiere Mortgage Originator in your area through hosting high value, education seminars for your local agents.

Simply put, *Instant Referrals*™ is the process of repeatedly attracting a targeted group of producing agents, packed into a room to hear a compelling topic and speaker (maybe you) during which you also get to present yourself, your value proposition and capture all the names, addresses, emails and phone numbers of every agent who attends.

You also get permission to follow-up, set meetings with agents you pre-select as 'worthy' and build relationships with those agents, converting them to referral partners (oil wells) in a systematic and predictable way.

Three Core Systems

My friend and colleague Michael E. Gerber is the bestselling author of <u>The E Myth; Why Most Small Businesses Don't Work and What to Do About It</u>. If you haven't read any of the books in the E Myth series – put them on your must read list today.

Michael and his consulting firm E Myth Worldwide have helped improve the lives of more than 3 million small business owners in over 160 countries during the last 30 years. What they've discovered is that for any business to realize its full potential it must have a clearly defined process for mastering these Three Core Systems.

1) Lead Generation

2) Lead Conversion

3) Client Fulfillment

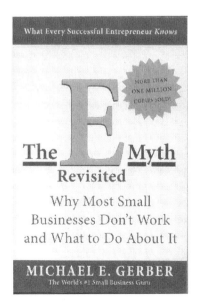

Most businesses tend to place the majority of their focus only on Lead Generation. Of course having a steady stream of qualified leads is vital for any business. However, too much focus on the top of the funnel without a process for nurturing and converting a percentage of leads over time costs you thousands is lost opportunity.

Salad vs. Garbage

There's an old saying that the difference between salad and garbage is timing. Mortgage Professionals mistakenly narrow their focus towards only those who are ready to 'buy now' or they get impatient if agents haven't referred a red-hot deal in the last thirty days.

They wind up frustrated having no consistency in fundings, feeling trapped and spinning their wheels every month to do it all over again. Keep in mind that people are ready to buy when they're ready to buy – not when you're ready for them to buy.

Real Estate agents are people too. Yes, shocking but true! Agents need to first trust you before they're comfortable and willing to send you a referral – which equates to their commission check, food on the table, education for their kids, mortgage payment and more.

You would be cautious about letting a complete stranger handle that too!

What's Your Process?

Have you ever visited a foreign country? Imagine for a moment that you're instantly transported a foreign city. You've never been there before, you have no map, don't know the language and your task is to get from point A to point B.

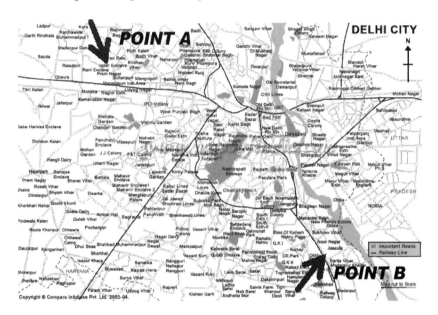

With no map, not knowing the language and being in a foreign country, how difficult would your task be? Of course you're smart and would attempt to get help along the way but let's face it – you would struggle, become frustrated and may even just give up at some point. If however you were handed a map and a language translation book, how much faster and with less struggle and frustration would you get from Point A to Point B?

That's right – a lot faster!

If you follow the steps outlined in this book, you will be equipped your map; a proven agent marketing system for:

1) Lead Generation (Capturing Agents)

2) Lead Conversion (Getting Referrals)

3) Client Fulfillment (Building Agent Loyalty)

A proven system that not only improves the quality and quantity of agents entering your funnel, but a system that finally delivers predictability of results that any well designed process should deliver.

Effectively positioning yourself through educational seminars for your local agents will have agents asking *you* to meet with *them*. You'll build agent relationships that are loyal and last for many years. You will start getting referrals from agents you never thought was possible!

Don't Believe a Word I Say!

You want to hear from an active Loan Officers who are actually cap-turing agents with little or no prospecting, having agents deliver buyer referrals every week on a silver platter – like clockwork?

Just log into your Free Gifts website for your Free Audio interviews. You'll learn more in these interviews than sitting through an entire seminar!

Listen to Free Audio interviews featuring
top producers reveal their success story. Visit:
www.GetInstantReferrals.com

The real 'secret' to your success with agents is when you have a 'system' or a process for finding, recruiting and nurturing agents; you'll expedite your results and reach that core number of agents you need to generate your closed loans each month.

Law of Large Numbers

The truth is that building a steady, stable, loyal group of agents who send you referrals each week on a silver platter is simply a numbers game. It's mathematics. I hated math during school but the good thing about math and formulas is that numbers don't lie. By using seminars as the top end of your agent marketing funnel, you're putting the law of large numbers to work – in your favor! Follow the formula and your results are predictable.

You're in total control!

When you finally realize that whoever gets in front of more agents, with a compelling offer and a system for converting those agents to referral partners – WINS!

It's called leverage. You already know that you're not going to convert 100% of your local agents to team up with you. They're either already loyal to another loan officer, married to one, *sleeping with one* or simply don't have any business to send you. Suddenly it becomes fun because it's like playing a game.

How many agents do *you* need to personally meet with in order to convert into 'oil wells' that actually produce closed loans for you?

Answer - a lot. You already know that the 80/20 rule exists in real estate like any other sales position, right? Knowing that's true, doesn't it make more sense to *speed-up* the process of meeting agents, qualifying and converting them into referral partners?

Reverse Prospecting

This new game is called Reverse Prospecting. When agents come out to see you, (and they will) attend your event, hear your information, you're no longer seen as "just another Loan Officer."

You've now turned the tables by becoming a source of relevant, problem solving content and resources for agents. You've positioned yourself as an expert and a professional vs. another Loan Officer scrounging around for the next handout from your local agent.

But, it is still is a numbers game - pure and simple. Whoever gets in front of the most agents – the "top 20%" and converts them – wins the game!

Kissing Toads

Here's the bottom line. If we as Mortgage Loan Officers recognize, accept, and acknowledge that we need real estate agents to be successful in this market, which is a purchase-dominant market, we're going to need to go through a lot of agents to find our core group of whatever your number happens to be. Today you need more agents than you did in the past.

core agents who refer to you one or two deals a month, at a bare minimum.

You're going to have to go through anywhere from fifty to one hundred agents just to find those core ten or twenty, to get the rapport, to have the synergy, to have the same kind of value match, to weed out the toxic agents and so on.

If that's the case, doing it any other way other than putting them in a room in a group format, is just insanity. It takes way too long to get there. What you're getting with seminars is... *speed*.

So let's say you get twenty agents at your first event. Then with a system for qualifying, converting to meetings and having a match, you get four of them become core players for you.

But that's only half of the story. Four become core players, but the truth of the matter is there will be agents who you keep in your email list for newsletters, video, on-going marketing, future seminar invites and more.

I can't tell you how many times in a given month I would get an agent just out of the blue who called me and said, "Hey Geoff, this is Susie Agent. I came to your seminar a month or two ago and haven't had a chance to talk to you, but I have a buyer. Can you help me with them?"

When properly applied, a front and back-end seminar system will *build residual benefits* as long as you stick with it and follow-up.

There's something uniquely powerful about a face-to-face, belly-to-belly event where agents are seeing how you present yourself, how knowledgeable you are, are you somebody I can feel confident in as either a) able to close my transaction, and b) can interact professionally with my clients? That's part of the secret sauce of that makes live seminars so powerful.

They can't get the same impact through Social Media. Of course Facebook should be an integral part of your overall agent seminar plan, but there is no substitute for in-person – especially because real estate is still a *local* business transaction. People buy homes from local agents and *local* Mortgage Professionals. That's what Chapter 3 is all about!

*"The person who gets the farthest is generally
the one who is willing to do and dare.
The sure-thing boat never gets far from shore."*

– Dale Carnegie

Chapter 3

Get Off Your Assets!

You're still with me – good! Most people never get beyond the first two chapters of a book so give yourself a high-five!

Are you beginning now to see the benefits and leverage of hosting seminars for agents to *speed up* your process for sifting and sorting through agents?

The mortgage meltdown and market shake-up over the last few years has revealed some truths about winning the game of being a Mortgage Professional. Most Loan Originators were riding high and experiencing success not necessarily because they diligently applied themselves in business building fundamentals but because the tide was rising everywhere.

When the tide rises, all the boats get lifted along with the tide. Virtually anyone can succeed when times are good. Lots of people believed during the recent boom years that they were the captain of the ship, that their results were achieved solely by charting their own success.

When times get tough and the tide goes out, suddenly things don't work like they used to. Quite a few get swept out to sea or wind up crashing into the rocks. We've seen plenty of that happen haven't we?

The recent market challenges have revealed the ugly truth and reality of what it takes to succeed long-term as a Mortgage Professional. It takes the right mindset and the right actions – consistently.

Top performers know it's never about the market. It's about what you *do* in the current market that determines your results. It's about knowing what to do and then actually doing it – repeatedly.

So here's a question for you:

"How many agents in your local area know that you exist?"

Do they know your name, your company, your voice, your personality; would they recognize you in a crowded room of agents and Mortgage Loan Officers?

Do they have *any* connection to you whatsoever beyond; "gee, I've seen her before, not sure who she is or what she does – I think she does loans."

Seriously – how many agents would know you beyond that level? Five? Ten? You already know that to build a stable, purchase money referral business you'll likely need to sort through at least one hundred agents to get your core ten or twenty – maybe more.

Get Into The Game

Where are sporting games played? On the field – right! Many Mortgage Loan Officers today aren't even on the field.

They're either sitting in the bleachers hoping to get noticed or, more often are sitting behind their computers on Email, Facebook or the latest bright and shiny object promising results without effort.

SPEED TIP

You will never build consistently loyal, profitable relationships with real estate agents without getting out in your local market, belly-to-belly, engaging, connecting and getting 'in the game' with your local agents.

If you think otherwise you're probably still struggling to capture more agents and get quality referrals.

So What Now?

Today's market is consistently moving from a refinance market to a purchase market. Forget that – it's already moved and most are playing catch up. Succeeding today means building quality relationships with producing real estate agents. We'll assume that you agree or you wouldn't have picked up this book and read this far. Keep reading – it gets even better!

The illustration represents two important elements. At the top is the Community of agents in your local area. At the bottom of the spiral is you – the circles represent the level of Awareness your local agent community has that you exist. The circles separating you from your local agent community are actions you must take to become known among your local agents to succeed with them.

You can see the circles include **Interaction, Engagement, Participation, Conversation** and **Affinity.** If you're going to be a real player and go after agent business, you've got to be engaged and participating in your local real estate community – period.

The Marketing **Spiral**

Community

Affinity

Conversation

Participation

Engagement

Interaction

© David // Armano   darmano.typepad.com

Awareness

Join Your Local Board

You will not succeed from a distance with agents. You must get up close and personal. That means, first of all, becoming an affiliate member of the local Board of REALTORS®. This is the local hub for agents and should be part of your strategy to get in the game.

If you become an affiliate member of the Board, you get on the newsletter, you may even get a list of all the members, you're now eligible to attend the local preview meetings where they announce the listings for sale, buyers, you can make special announcements, be a guest speaker offering mortgage related updates, promote yourself and get the sheet of hot listings – so you can work up finance flyers and offer them to listing agents when you preview their listing on Broker Preview day. I can guarantee you that your competitors are attending these weekly meetings. It's a worthwhile exercise simply to size up what other lenders are participating in these meetings, what their approach and involvement level is and what you can do differently to capture the agent's attention.

✳ Success Story #1 ✳

Tripled Agent Attendance At Seminars

My friend and Mortgage Originator Brian Kludt is a Senior Mortgage Planner and Branch Manager with Waterstone Mortgage in Menomonee Falls, Wisconsin.

He's experienced at hosting monthly agent seminars with his Steep & Brew events that attract local agents to come learn business building tips, latest mortgage happenings and more.

"By simply joining my local Board of REALTORS® I boosted my average attendance at my seminars from about 15 agents to over 80 agents at each seminar!"

Brian Kludt – Senior Mortgage Planner
Waterstone Mortgage

Well Known vs. Highly Knowledgeable

What's more important to your success as a Mortgage Professional – being well known or being extremely knowledgeable?

Of course having knowledge about underwriting guidelines, products, interest rates and the latest regulations affecting mortgage and real estate markets is critical.

Have you ever seen an agent or a Mortgage Professional who has less knowledge and less experience out-produce someone with more experience and more knowledge?

Why?

Because knowledge only becomes useful when it's applied! If you've got a wealth of knowledge but don't have the exposure and awareness in your market to engage people in your services – you lose by default.

Hosting your own educational seminars is the one-two punch that will make you well known and make it known that you are knowledge. Both are important assets to your immediate and long-term success.

*"My success, part of it certainly, is that
I have focused in on a few things."*

– Bill Gates

Chapter 4

Getting Started
With Seminars

By now you're probably at one of three points of interest in
hosting educational seminars for your local agents.

1) Yes! I agree agent seminars are a quicker, faster and
    better method for finding and converting agents to
    referral partners.

2) I agree it makes sense, I just don't know if they'll
    work for me – I need help!

3) I've tried seminars in the past and wasn't thrilled
    with the results.

If you're at number one, keep reading because this book is your blueprint to get started *fast* and get the results you want *fast*.

If you're at number two, you're in the right place at the right time! The following chapters take you step-by-step through the entire process of hosting agent seminars from soup to nuts. Regardless of your experience, your market or your budget, everything you need to get started and look good is right here.

If you're at number three, you'll really enjoy what's next because most Loan Officers who host agent seminars are missing at least three critically important parts that hinder attendance numbers, minimize the quality of agents who attend and greatly diminish their results.

The Fear of Speaking

If you're one of those people who like what you hear so far, you like all the advantages and benefits of doing seminar marketing, but you're still a little bit queasy, a little hesitant, and a little fearful about the idea of stepping up and speaking in front of a group, you're in good company!

I've had the privilege of sharing the stage with some pretty big names including: Tony Robbins, Michael Gerber, Brian Tracy, Jack Canfield and Mark Victor Hansen – co creators of the Chicken

Soup for the Soul books which have now sold over 500 million copies worldwide (to name just a few).

Each one of them has told me they still get nervous energy before giving a presentation and I do too. The point is that it's ok; you'll survive and gain more mastery of yourself each time you speak in front of a group.

If you're going to be a top performer you simply have to get used to speaking in public. You've just got to get over it, get through it, and do it. You don't have to be as entertaining as Elvis returned from the grave. You just need to be yourself, be authentic, have a plan and take action!

Having Others Speak With You

You remember Chapter Three and the Marketing Spiral and benefits of joining your local Board of REALTORS® Association? Here's another benefit to joining: You begin to network with, get access to other **S**ubject **M**atter **E**xperts (SME's) who you can team-up with to jointly present relevant content for your local agents.

You can find a list of SME's who are also affiliate members of your local Board of REALTORS® on a variety of topics like local Tax experts, Financial Planning, Social Media and marketing experts. All you do is walk into your Board of REALTORS® and ask them where to find those people, or join the Board and you'll get the list!

You can see who is advertising and whose writing articles in their publication. They always have a quarterly or a monthly publication.

They also usually have monthly meetings, annual trade shows and conventions you can go to and see who's exhibiting at the booths. There's lots of ways to find out who is providing products and services to REALTORS® that you can partner with and do alliances with to have as potential co-speakers and seminar sponsors.

SME Guest Speaker Topics:

* Staging Your Listings For Top Dollar

* Social Media Success In 30 Minutes Per Day

* Going From Credit Repair To Approved Buyer

* Video Marketing For Agents Made Easy

SPEED TIP

Here's a novel idea. Call the agents you already know and ask them. "Hey, what areas of your business are most important to you right now? What areas do you need more assistance in?" Send out a survey from SurveyMonkey.com and get feedback. They'll tell you the areas, and then you go find those resources among your local affiliate members team-up and provide those solutions to your agents through educational seminars.

Billion Dollar Agents ~ Lessons Learned

The top three things that you should always keep in mind about agents are:

1.   They want to attract more quality listings/buyers.

2.   They want to sell homes faster and for top dollar with fewer struggles.

3.   They want to stay current on what's working in today's market and how they can apply tools and systems in their business.

Myself and Walter Sanford at Our Agent Seminar

This is what I learned from Walter Sanford. Walter a top agent, held the record of selling a home a day, every day – for sixteen years in a row. He's sold over $1 Billion in homes and today coaches some of the top agents in the country.

If you can deliver content in the form of educational training that hits any or all of those three hot buttons, you've got a pretty strong chance of hitting a home run and getting agents lining up to attend your event and build a mutually profitable relationship with you – because you're adding value to their bottom line. That alone set you apart from most of your competition who are still showing up with their hand out – asking for a loan.

Small Is Big

Getting started is easy. Start with a 60-90 minute presentation and bring in somebody else to help you – a co-presenter, an affiliate sponsor that makes compliments your topic, title, home inspection, warranty, pests, whatever, and get them to take a portion of the presentation as well, so you're not on the spot for the entire time. It's okay to have handouts and read some notes from your handouts and look at your PowerPoint slides up on the screen.

You really need to just get started. Like riding a bike, eventually is gets easier and soon you'll remove the training wheels and cruising along, enjoying the ride!

SPEED TIP

• *Be Prepared: You don't want to read from a script or come across boring or uninformed about your topic. Know your subject so well that you don't need slides or notes. The slides are there just to keep you on track.*

• *Be Authentic: Speak from the heart and be yourself. People respond to honest authority. You're not selling your sharing, educating and empowering with information and your focus on impacting people.*

• *Engage Your Audience: You're not giving a lecture. You're conducting an interactive workshop. Let your audience know you want them to participate, ask questions and take notes.*

Just remember that presenting in front of small groups of agents is easy to get started. You don't have to go it alone; agents will appreciate your knowledge, your authenticity and your desire to sincerely help will go further than any script or cheesy canned lecture.

WOW! Factor Seminars

Let's talk about what topics to actually bring REALTORS® in the door and get butts in the seats. There is a benchmark or criteria that you must know and adhere to for best results. You've got to put the REALTORS® cap on and ask yourself:

> *"If I'm an agent, why would I care about learning more about this topic?"*

Remember, our lesson from Walter Sanford?

Agents are primarily interested in three areas:

1. They want to attract more quality listings/buyers.

2. They want to sell homes faster and for top dollar with fewer struggles.

3. They want to stay current on what's working in today's market and how they can leverage tools, systems and knowledge to grow.

Now, within each of these areas are a bunch of topics and subjects that properly positioned and promoted effectively, will get you superb results at your seminars that lead to relationships and referrals – **guaranteed!**

You also don't have to come up with all of this content on your own. You'll be partnering with other Affiliate Members, inviting Subject Matter Experts (SME's) etc. You'll never run out of topics or content to present when you team up with others.

Here are a few more actual seminar topics and titles that capture agents' attention and get butts in the seats.

- **Gain the Inside Edge – Secrets of America's Top Producers**

- **YouTube for Real Estate Agents**

- **Survival of the Fittest – How Top Agents Tackle Tough Times**

- **5 Steps To Getting Referrals On Facebook for Real Estate Agents**

- **Top 10 Web Tools for Real Estate Agents**

- **Getting Started With Social Media**

The list can go on and on. Just understand what it is that agents are struggling with, what areas they need help with, and then you craft a presentation around that.

And remember, you don't have to be the subject matter expert in the topic, nor do you have to be the only presenter to feel like all the pressure is on you. You can have guest presenters assist you in your presentation. Maybe they know more about a particular topic that you want to present.

You invite them out to present and usually they do it for free because they get additional exposure for their own business.

You may want to consider hiring guest speakers for a fee who are experts in certain topics as necessary.

Getting Paid Speakers

When you're ready, you may want to consider hiring a speaker, author or trainer who charges a fee to speak. Of course, you can be very successful just hosting your own events with your own local speakers, but if you have an interest in hosting even larger events and creating a huge buzz, do your research and select a speaker appropriate for your market and audience.

You can contact us for a free consultation to learn more here: geoff@GetInstantReferrals.com

Where To Host Your Seminars

It's the old real estate adage; location, location, location. The first place I always look to hold an event first is at the local Board of REALTORS®. If the facility is large enough and has a room that can hold at least twenty people or more, and it's an affordable rental rate, then that's the very first place I would always hold my seminars, unless they outgrew the capacity.

Why there? It's neutral ground. They're used to coming there. For most, it's a friendly, familiar, welcoming place. It's not your office, which sometimes can be a barrier to overcome, so that would be the first place.

Also, if it's a free event – sometimes the local Board will even help you promote it and get the word out through their email blasts and things like that, so you've got another leverage point.

It's another reason to join the Board!

You'll develop some relationships with the folks inside and sometimes they can help you out, so that's number one venue.

Next on your list are community centers, a local college, executive suites or restaurants. Those are usually very inexpensive, and come audiovisual-equipped, meaning they've got the sound, the screen, whatever you need to present audio and visual.

SPEED TIP

Whatever venue you choose, you want to make sure that it's not sequestered off in some remote, unknown area of your local community that people don't know how to get to very easily.

As you know, people are directionally-challenged, agents in particular. You just want to remove as many potential hurdles as you can to having people show up at your event, so make sure your venue is known by your local agents and easy to drive to.

Last on the list, but still very viable and good choices are hotels. That's not to say that a hotel doesn't make sense. It oftentimes does, depending on the size of the audience you might have and costs. In your area, hotels may be a bargain. In New York City – not so much. Do you have sponsors who are helping you pay for the event to offset your costs? If your budget allows and your sponsor help defer costs – go for it!

Start small and reasonable in the beginning. If you book a large room wind up having mostly empty seats, it leaves a negative impression, a negative vibe. There's something powerful about being 'sold out' – at max capacity!

Social Proof

Which restaurant is you more compelling to eat at – the one that's empty on Friday night at 7:00PM or the one with a line out the door and a 40 minute wait?

People want to go where other people are going and people are attracted to those who have perceived influence over others. It's a concept discussed at length in the book <u>Influence</u> by Dr. Robert Cialdini. Social proof is a powerful element of promoting events and building instant credibility in your local market with agents.

Agents can't see that you have attracted room full of REALTORS® when you send them a postcard, an email or when you cold-call them on the phone.

But when they come to your event and see that you actually have other agents showing up…*Shazam!*

Suddenly you have authority, you have positioning, you have posture, and you're instantly magnetic!

KLT Factor

What's your KLT factor? You've heard it said that for agents to send you referrals they have to:

1) **Know You**

2) **Like You**

3) **Trust You**

Hosting live seminars for your local agents is the most effective and fastest way to establish and boost your **KLT** Factor.

Yes, faster and more effective than Facebook, Twitter, LinkedIn or video. Nothing accelerates your personal influence, likeability and trust faster than face-to-face, personal engagement – nothing!

✳ Success Story #2 ✳

Craig Sewing is an award winning all star originator and team leader. He's also the host of the Craig Sewing's "Real Talk" daily radio show in San Diego, CA.

Craig started out hosting small educational events for his local agents and has since grown his attendance to hundreds of agents at each of his events, generating a 100% high volume refer-ral business.

Want to hear how he does it?

Your Free Audios and bonuses are waiting for you at:
www.GetInstantReferrals.com

Life responds to deserve and not to need. It doesn't say, "If you need, you will reap." It says, "If you plant you will reap. " The guy says, "I really need to reap. "Then you really need to plant."

– Jim Rohn

Chapter 5

Getting Butts In Seats

Now, how do we get agents to actually show up? It all starts with your *topic*. What's the compelling headline, offer or reason to attend your event? It's got to be something that stops them in their tracks, captures their attention and has them saying…"this is for me!"

Earlier we mentioned that many Loan Officers who attempt to host seminars for agents wind up disappointed with the attendance. Usually, poor attendance is just a symptom of a larger problem – which can be cured.

Does your event, the title, copy and marketing collateral (online and offline) address one or all of our four key factors for agents we learned earlier?

Shock and Awe

That means when you launch a "shock and awe" marketing campaign that goes both wide and deep. You involve other people to assist you in carrying out your mission. People like Title, Escrow, Home Inspection, Home Warranty, Insurance, Appraisers and other affiliate members of your local Board.

Why involve others like Title, Escrow and Home Warranty? Because these reps are in the real estate offices every single day, they have access to the closed offices, top producers and key influencers.

Your Unpaid Sales Force

Affiliates like Title, Escrow, Home Warranty and others are as my friend and Coach Tim Davis refers to as; "your unpaid sales force." They will help you get the word out about your seminar – at no cost to you. Some of these affiliates will likely even become sponsors of your event, helping you cover your costs!

Even with tighter rules placed on Title companies, most will still hand out your seminar flyers for you to agents and offices they see every day. They just want something that will add value to their real estate agents' business as well, just like you do.

They're going to be your salespeople, your boots on the ground, handing out hundreds of flyers for you to offices you would otherwise never get into. So that's number one. Find good affiliates or other people to help you promote the event.

Event Marketing with Facebook

1) I recommend having your own event registration page outside of Facebook. Use a free site like www. eventbrite.com It integrates directly into Facebook and provides superior tracking and promotion related tools – free!

   The more Facebook Likes, Twitter retweets, LinkedIn shares etc. on your blog posts and web pages the more visitors will perceive your content or seminar as being popular and will also want to share. The best place to position your social share buttons is at the top "above the fold" (visible without scrolling).

   Add the following social share buttons to your event registration page if possible:

   * TweetMeme Retweet Button

   * Facebook Like Button

   * LinkedIn Share Button

2) Add a blurb to your Facebook Page banner.

The image on your Facebook Page is prime real estate. Consider using your page image/banner with a link to get on a list to be notified of free seminars etc. You could also add images about the event to your Page to go across the top of your page with calls to action.

3) Promote your registration page on your Page wall.
You can periodically promote the direct link to your event – perhaps with a question – something like "Have you got your ticket yet to this exciting event?" or "Hands up who's attending this?!"

4) Create a Facebook Event. This is one of the most abused and misunderstood features of Facebook.

There are basically two ways to create an Event on Facebook:
- **On your personal Profile and**
- **On your Page. (Formerly Fan Page).**

I strongly suggest you create a Facebook Event via your Page for any business-related events and keep the personal/social events for your Profile. Just click the Events link on the left of your Page, then click the "Create an Event" button.

One thing to note about Facebook Events, you'll want to make it really clear there is a link that Facebook users need to click in order to register. Some people might think that by clicking the "I'm Attending" button they have signed up for your event; they haven't. Write periodic updates and messages on the Event wall to encourage everyone to go get their ticket or register via your external registration page or website if they haven't already.

Also, the Event photo/graphic is one of the most important features – when users share the Event around Facebook, the thumbnail of the image goes with it.

5) Offer live micro events on your Page. One great way to build buzz for your events is to host "Expert Fridays" where a subject matter expert spends one hour answering questions directly on the fan Page wall. Th is helps to introduce yourself or any guest speakers, provides tremendous value, and helps to build your social equity.

6) Encourage attendees to engage and share. Once participants have signed up for your event, encourage them to write on your Facebook Event wall and engage through other social channels.

Email Marketing

Building or obtaining a good email list of local agents will do wonders for you. Of course you want to comply with CAN-SPAM rules when sending emails to those who have not previously opted in and agreed to receive email from you.

A simple way around that is to have a web page or section of your blog or Facebook or Twitter offering to update agents on trainings or events in your local that they might be interested in attending.

SPEED TIP

If you are looking for good sources of email lists of agents, I've found a couple of decent websites, and there are different ways to use them.

One is called www.eCampaignPro.com. That's an e-flyer distribution service to share property flyers with other agents that goes to all the different agents. You can pull agent lists by zip code, county, whatever you want. You can also send e-Flyer announcements on any topic to agents in targeted zip codes.

Another resource you may want to try if you want to purchase a list of local agents either by zip code, local board members, county, state – they have it all! Just go to: www.Real-Estate-Agent-Lists.com

You can just pay for their email and their name, or other data and it's quite affordable and accurate. This is the only company I've found, other than www.realtor.org that has a scrubbed, current, and up-to-date list.

Just remember, the most important thing to your seminar success is to have a compelling seminar title. Just like a book. When you get a best-selling book they don't say it's on the "best-written" book list. They say it's on the best-selling book list. The title sells the book and a compelling, benefit driven title will sell your seminar – and get agents attending in droves.

Co-Sponsors

I never do a seminar without a co-sponsor, and that doesn't always mean somebody I'm getting money from, but often it does.

What are the advantages to getting a co-sponsor? We'll get to money as the number two advantage. First and foremost I believe the advantage to an appropriate co-sponsor is exposure to agents I would otherwise not get exposure to.

You already learned how title and escrow companies can be your 'boots on the ground" getting access into offices and in front of agents that are closed and supposedly untouchable. Maybe it's attorneys if you've got what's called a wet state, where attorneys actually handle the closing instead of escrow.

There's home warranty. Everybody's got a home warranty; I don't care where you are in North America. That's another great partner. Why? Because every house that somebody buys needs a home warranty on it. The agents are interacting with these home warranty reps on a regular basis.

To find great co-sponsors, check out some of your local listings. The local magazines, Homes & Land, Harmon Homes, and whatever else you have that are actually advertising homes on behalf of agents can be another great sponsor.

Anybody that has a vested interest in getting in front of real estate agents can include:

- Home inspectors

- Home repair

- Tax planners

- Financial advisors

- Marketing Firms

- 1031 Exchange Firms

- Transaction Coordinators

- Home Staging

- Property Inspection

- Web Design Firms

- Storage Facilities

- Insurance

Getting Co-Sponsor Money

You want to set a fee structure making it easy for your potential sponsors to evaluate the cost and benefits of getting involved with your seminar. Having three different sponsor levels outlined on a single-sided flyer with dollar amounts and benefits at each level works just fine.

Get your FREE Sponsor Enrollment Form
www.GetInstantReferrals.com

Hopefully, you already with work title, home warranty, appraisal, escrow and more affiliates who refer you agents and vice versa. If not, it's a great opportunity to create additional business for all. If you get enough affiliates involved, the fees for the event can be spread across several sponsors, versus just two or three main sponsors.

Getting Co-Sponsors Promoting

- Lender, Title, Escrow as main sponsors and they take lion's share of responsibilities related to venue location, event promotion, and costs.

- Each of the main sponsors must equally share promotion of event and get buy-in from senior management at each company. A conference call is a good way to bring everyone together to cover strategy, tactics and issue marching orders.

- Furthermore, bi-weekly sales or conference call meetings should include "from the street" updates, list share and head count update.

- Include all other relevant sponsors to help offset costs such as Home Warranty, Appraisal, Pest/Termite, Homes & Land, Harmon Homes, Attorneys, etc.

SPEED TIP

A contest for reps at sponsoring companies with the most guests helps to drive activity – especially for sales oriented sponsors who are money or prize motivated.

Be sure to look-up the list of affiliate members of your local Board to find event sponsors. Your local Board of REALTORS® is also a potential sponsor. They may agree to help you promote your event and even waive or discount the room rental and services fee because you're helping to educate their agent members.

Another great reason to join your local board!

We've talked about the basics of agent seminars, such as getting agents butts in seats, getting started, teaming up with other affiliates and how to get sponsors to pay for your event.

There are of course several moving parts that must work together – like the pit crew of a Formula 1 race team – to ensure your event is a success. Let's review.

What Are Your Costs?

You will incur some expenses. You can't avoid that. To make money, sometimes you have to invest money. While the obvious may not need to be listed here, other expenses you may incur in are the following:

- Venue / Room Rental

- Food / Beverages

- Audio / Visual

- Promotion / Marketing / Advertising

- Invitations / Flyers / Tickets

- Logistics / Reservations / Confirmations

It is possible to have a good portion or all of these expenses covered by getting co-sponsors for your event such as Title, Escrow, Home Warranty, Inspection, Appraisal, Homes & Land, etc. as mentioned in the previous chapter.

When To Hold Your Event

The date you are going to have this event should include six weeks minimum lead time for marketing; the date should be cleared with any guest speakers, and, most importantly, should be available with the hotel or venue.

Believe it or not, these rooms book up quickly. If possible, pick a day without competing programs, property preview tours, or seminars for real estate agents as best as you can. Most events begin at 9:00AM or 10:00AM or a lunch session beginning at 11:30 or 12:00 for approximately 90 minutes.

Advertising and Marketing

When designing promotional materials for your event, it's important to remember the following:

- Flyers should be high quality and full color. It must include a compelling, benefit driven headline or seminar title and a clear call to action for reservations.

- Print up a small quantity (100) of event tickets to be used for VIP REALTOR® invitations to create some exclusivity and boost 'show rates.'

Taking Seminar Reservations

My experience is that if you can automate the process of taking reservations, do it. If you're using email to promote your event, you'll need to provide a webpage where people can make reservations.

SPEED TIP

A great resource for setting up a seminar RSVP page is www.EventBrite.com It's free because your events are free. If you're charging for the event, then they take a certain percentage of each ticket you sell.

It's a great platform because it allows you to integrate a Google map to the location, you can upload custom HTML pages, and you can E-mail reminders using their system, print name badges and print the RSVP list – all FREE!

The system even allows your agents to instantly print an admission ticket when they make a reservation on www.EventBrite.com

I've found it to be the best darn thing out there, aside from building your own custom page.

You and your co-sponsors will be promoting your event with flyers and email – and Facebook. We'll go into more details on effectively using Facebook to promote your events later.

You'll get some who simply prefer to RSVP with a quick phone call which is why you need to provide at least two ways to register. It's nearly impossible to have a person waiting idle to jump on the phone if and when a reservation call comes in. It's costly and unproductive.

Besides, calls come in at all hours and your response rates increase with a 24 hr. reservation line.

When taking phone reservations you have three options

1) Use an existing staff person, assistant or someone else to stand by the phones 24/7 waiting for calls to come is at all hours. I do not recommend this as an option. For the simple fact that agents will call at all hours to make a reservation and no one person can handle that, you will lose lots of people if they are left to fend for themselves in a company voice mail system.

2) Take advantage of the technology many agents already use everyday – call capture.

3) On your flyer, postcard or invitation, include the following verbiage: To RSVP Call 1-800-123-4567 Ext. 200 / 24 Hr Recorded Message. This is a very easy, simple and inexpensive method for capturing reservations and phone numbers of agents reserving seats. You still have to follow-up with them and confirm their attendance at least three times prior to your event date.

4) Outsource the entire process of speaker selection, event logistics, reservations, confirmation, follow-up, list management, marketing, promotion, etc.

SPEED TIP

Have either you or your guest speaker call in and record message for the 24 Hr. RSVP recorded message, getting people pumped up as they make their reservation – boosting your show rates. Of course, call capture saves the phone number of the person calling but make sure your message requests they leave their name, number, company name and email address for follow-up. You'll want all that information for proper follow-up.

Sample Voicemail Script:

"Hello and thank you for calling to reserve your seat for (Your Seminar Title). At the tone, please leave your name, any guest's names and your telephone number and email address for confirmation. Please speak slowly and spell any unusual names. You will receive a confirmation that your seats are reserved. For more information visit: (Your Event Website) or call us at: 867-5309. We look forward to seeing you there!

Getting email addresses is critical! It's the simplest and cheapest way to confirm their reservation and send reminders, as you get closer to your event. You can even use it as a viral campaign offering rewards for people to forward the invitation to another agent they know.

Voice Broadcast

Another technology available is using voice broadcast to send a single message to your reservation list at one time. It saves you the time of calling each person directly (which I still recommend if possible) while allowing you to again promote the event and have your attendees invite other agents. You can also have the speaker do a "live update" message as the event draws near, creating renewed enthusiasm and commitment to attend.

Food

Remember, the event is largely about creating a perception that you are a class act, including the common courtesy to serve some refreshments for your attendees. For morning events, provide a simple assortment of donuts or muffins, juice, water and coffee. For mid-day perhaps some cookies, granola bars or fruit.

A simple and cost effective way to provide food, juice and water for your attendees is to visit your local Costco, Sam's or other similar type store and buy your basic items there. You can get muffins, donuts, cookies, bottled water or whatever in quantity at very reasonable prices.

Coffee

Would you invite a hungry, tired, angry bear to your seminar? If you don't provide coffee for your morning seminar, that's exactly what you'll get – tired, hungry bears that get very angry without their coffee!

We hosted one event where on of our co-sponsors was responsible for bringing the coffee. They decided to blow it off – "not that big of a deal" they said.

Grrrrrrrrrr!

That's the sound the tired, angry bears make when they arrive at your morning event to discover there is no coffee – yikes! Providing coffee is an absolute *must* for morning events.

Even afternoon events because a little caffeine is good for the soul – and helps to ensure they stay awake!

Serving cookies or snacks for afternoon events will pay huge dividends in maximizing your agents positive experience; making you and your company that much more memorable.

SPEED TIP

Get your co-sponsors to help defray or subsidize the cost. There are many ways to divide the costs related to a seminar like other affiliates or those you send referrals to; they owe you!

*"You've got to go out on a limb sometimes
because that's where the fruit is."*

– Will Rogers

Chapter 6

It's Showtime!

The Day of Your Event

There's a lot to do on the day of your event. I recommend you arrive 90 minutes early to ensure proper room set-up, testing of AV equipment, rehearsing your presentation and reviewing your objectives with any speaker and others involved in promoting the event.

The day of the event is about being visible, meeting as many agents as you can and thanking your existing agents for coming. Be sure to have welcome tables with staff to sign people in and distribute materials. It's also helpful to have other staff scattered about the room to ensure people are taking their seats, networking, enjoying some refreshments and enjoying themselves.

Setting The Stage

The room should be abuzz with energy and upbeat music to facilitate networking and conversation. For some agents, this will be like homecoming having not seen each other in some time.

You should allow approximately thirty to sixty minutes from your stated check-in time to start time for your seminar to begin. This allows ample time for those arriving on time to eat and mingle. You will have agents showing up "casually late." That's to be expected. Keep someone at the registration table for thirty minutes after your seminar start time to handle those stragglers.

Your Welcome Message

When you see that most people have begun to eat, and it's just about time to begin, simply make a five minute warning announcement which will allow them to take their seats and prepare for the speaker. Stay on schedule as much as possible. For those who arrive late, that's their problem. You'll find that most people arrive on time and respect the fact that you start on time as well.

Have an introduction prepared and be sure to acknowledge all parties involved in making your event a success. Keep it brief and simple. The agents came to hear about the main topic not a co-sponsor drone on forever.

You and your co-sponsor affiliates should have a designated three "commercial" either at the beginning of the event or after people return from the break if one is given. You can also present your "commercial" or call to action about doing business together at the close of your session – after you've built tremendous value with your seminar content.

Again, keep the commercial brief, upbeat and on pace. I recommend no one other than you or your guest speaker should have the floor longer than three to five minutes - max.

You may want to do a raffle to collect business cards and create some excitement in the room. If the speaker has products, you can raffle off a product or offer a discount on your lender fees, free appraisal, book, gift card or whatever. The raffle helps to create energy, break the ice and position you effectively.

Getting Agent Appointments

In Chapter Two we looked at your Three Core Systems from Michael Gerber's book The E-Myth:

1) **Lead Generation (More Agents)**

2) **Lead Conversion (More Buyer Referrals)**

3) **Client Fulfillment (More Agent Loyalty)**

Step one of course is Lead Generation with seminars as our main system for efficiently reaching more agents, faster. The next step is equally critical – if not more so. No sense in going through all the effort of hosting seminars for agents if you have no idea of how to convert your attendees into referral partners right? Here's where most Originators and mortgage companies miss the mark. They get a bunch of agents in a room and the seminar ends with the usual "thank you for coming" and round of applause – yippee!

Huh?

What a waste of time and money. You're not hosting a "warm fuzzy" session, holding hands and singing Kumbaya! Your objective is to capture and convert. Carpe Diem!

Lead Conversion

Some of the Agents who attend your seminar will already be looking for a quality Mortgage Originator like yourself. They don't carry a sign, they aren't wearing funny hats and they won't tell you unless you do one thing:

How do you ask a room full of agents if they're happy with their current lender or if they're looking for a lender – namely you?

Seminar Feedback Form

Also known as: *"The Agent Appointment Setting Form;"* this form will tell you exactly who's interested in talking with you and who you will be calling first in your follow-up calls.

The Seminar Feedback Form is designed to achieve three things:

1) Get feedback on what agents liked about your seminar and other topics they would be interested in learning more about at future seminars.

2) Discover which areas of their business are most critical for them right now – what areas are they struggling?

3) Are they happy with their current lender and/or are they open to meeting with you to learn more about how you can help them achieve their goals.

Get Your Free Seminar Feedback Form At: www.GetInstantReferrals.com

Getting agents to raise their hand and tell you if they're open to working with you using this form is simple.

Here's What You Say

At the conclusion of your seminar, you simply want to wrap up with the following sample script:

> *"Thank you all for coming today. By a show of hands, how many of you feel your time was well spent and you learned some things you can apply to your business? Great! Our goal in hosting this event is to add value to our local real estate community. Would you like to receive updates on future events like this? Great, we would love to have you back and invite your colleagues.*
>
> *We also want your feedback on how to improve, what topics you're most interested in and what areas of your business we might be able to help you with. We have a Feedback Form that will help us know what areas are most important to you and how we can help. Before you leave, would you help us by completing the form because we have a special gift for you as our appreciation for you attending today and for completing the Feedback Form and turning it in on your way out."*

You want to have some kind of a free gift like a Free Report, eBook, CD, coupon, presentation of value in return for your attendees completing the Feedback Form. You can either give it to them right there or tell them you'll send it to them within the next few days – setting the stage for a follow-up call. This Appointment Setting Form will come in handy when making follow-up calls to your agents.

People are willing to complete a short survey or questionnaire when you position it correctly and offer a thank you gift for taking a few extra minutes.

Now you've successfully promoted and filled an event with agents, many who, prior to the event, had no relationship with you at all. Well that's all changed now hasn't it?

Their attendance at your event gives you the right and responsibility to follow up with them, doing everything in your power to become their preferred lender of choice.

Remember, the goal of your event should be:

- Establish your presence among the REALTOR® community, positioning yourself as a leading authority.

- Create a high content, low "pitch" event that adds value and generates a "buzz"

- Deliver your "Value Added" commercial in 3 – 5 minutes max!

- Collect agents' contact information for database building and drip campaign follow-up.

- Set meetings with agents by using the Seminar Feedback Form.

Free Stuff For Your Agents!

Smart Loan Officers are always looking for ways to add value to agents beyond the usual "great rates and service" which, as you know, doesn't even begin to position you as unique and different.

One effective strategy is to have a post event "stick" system or platform to stay connected to your agents, continually adding value to their business. Ideally, you would have such a 'system' already in place, ready to go during your seminar. That way you capitalize on the energy and momentum while it's fresh during your seminar and agents are excited.

Announcing TopAgent TV!

We've created a private membership site for Mortgage Originators customized with your personal brand where agents must go through you to get access online videos, top agent interviews, marketing downloads, webinars, Social Media training and more.

You build tremendous loyalty with agents when you help them achieve their goals and overcome their business challenges. You'll find free stuff for your agents as giveaways, loyalty programs and more to help you convert more agents to loyal referral partners.

It's called TopAgent TV and you can see a brief video overview and learn more by going here:

www.TopAgentTV.com

"One-half of life is luck; the other half is discipline and that's the important half, for without discipline you wouldn't know what to do with luck."

– Carl Zuckmeyer

Chapter 7

The 'F' Word

It's usually "the weakest link" of most Originators entire business. What's the 'F' Word?

You guessed it - **Follow-Up!**

By implementing seminars, you'll be following-up on *warm* leads versus cold calling, open houses and all those other low pay-off, manual labor activities. You must be prepared to capitalize on the large numbers of agents you'll be meeting.

The seminars you host become the entry point of your Agent marketing funnel. You must have the systems, processes, and diligence through all the steps in your marketing funnel so out the other end of the funnel, oil wells of producing Agents with purchase money referrals will feed you for life.

The 'secret' to creating new, moneymaking relationships from your event is not simply in following-up with the attendees. Anyone can make a phone call and thank him or her for attending. Your goal is to leverage off the energy generated by the event and capitalize on their perception of you as someone offering more than just great rates and service.

You are now transformed in their eyes. You're no longer just a Loan Officer. You're a leading authority and a valuable asset to their business. But, agents have a short attention span and need to be reminded, constantly, that you are not like all the other Mortgage Loan Officers calling on them. So how do you turn your list of attendees into a recurring stream of referrals?

Most people buy after 7 contacts from a business, most businesses stop marketing after 3 contacts.

The Fortune Is In the Follow-Up!

You are now sitting on a goldmine (or should I say oil well) because you now have all these names, numbers and email addresses of agents that attended your event, got to know you and understand that you offer way more than what those 'other' Loan Officers in town offer. You are on the cusp of reaching new heights of influence and production in your business.

Now that you have all these names and addresses, what do you DO with them? Ahhh, grasshopper … you market your pants off to get meetings and build new relationships with these agents! Of course, you already knew that, didn't you?

If done correctly, you'll naturally get meetings, loans and new referral partners simply by hosting your own seminars. But you'll be leaving a *lot* of money on the table if you don't effectively and consistently *follow-up* with each and every attendee.

Instant Referrals™ Follow-Up System

- Personal Thank You email on the day of event – Close the email with a mention of personal meetings, free gift promised at event etc.

- Personal Thank You call day after the event. Close the call using the Seminar Feedback Form and referencing the Agents comments on the form and book meetings for a two week window.

- Guest Speaker email or voice broadcast Thank You within 2-3 days following event – Cross promote lender/sponsors/recommend agents to accept your call and meeting.

- Thank You card/letter to arrive within 3-5 days following event.

- Begin drip campaign within 3-5 days after event – Includes postcards, emails, CD's newsletter, voice broadcast, etc.

- Conduct seminars monthly, every other month or quarterly to build momentum, local and a buzz among your local agent community.

SPEED TIP

Depending on the speaker and topic, you can even host a post-event, follow-up group-coaching program for the key agents.

I've done this with real estate trainers because the agents appreciate extra attention and help implementing marketing ideas into their business.

We had a group of ten core agents go through a four week FSBO and Expired's tele-coaching program with top agent and trainer Walter Sanford which made me look like a hero, cost the agents nothing and created a huge feeling of reciprocation on the agent's part that compelled them into sending me business.

You can do the same whether your seminar topic was about 203K Loans, Marketing Tools, Social Media, whatever.

It's what happens after your event
that determines your success!

Post-event follow-up is **critical**. You must strike while the iron is **hot**! Agents have an attention span of a gnat and quickly move onto other things. If you let them cool off too long, your job becomes a lot harder getting back in front of them again. That's why you **must** act fast and follow-up within the first 24 hours of your event. The clock is ticking!

✳Success Story #3 ✳

"We set meetings with 19 Agents within a few days of the seminar!" We had 170 registrants and 84 who showed up. Of those roughly 46 agents checked the please contact me box on the survey form. My partner Tom has been following up and so far has 19 appointments, one of them with a "Top 20" agent who has 115 listings and funds more than $20 million annually. All the agents loved it and can't wait for the next one."

PaulDunn
Sunstreet Mortgage
Tucson, AZ

Striking Oil With Agents

Here's how to set meetings with agents following your seminar. Using your Seminar Feedback Form, you call those agents who requested your 'free gift' offered at the close of your event using this sample script:

Appointment Setting Script

"Hello, Mr. / Mrs. Big Time Agent," this is (Your Name/Company). You recently attended our seminar (Insert Title). First I wanted to thank you for attending. We're reviewing the feedback forms and noticed that you said it was great and you wanted to be notified of future events. You also checked that yes, you wanted a copy of this free CD, Report, Book, Gift…etc."

"I have your free gift right here. When do you think we can briefly get together so I can give you your (free gift) and review how you can apply one or two of the ideas from the seminar to your business?"

Boom!

Now you've scheduled yourself an appointment! You're Seminar Feedback Form is actually a…Agent Appointment-Setting Form!

Cool – huh?

Of course there are lots of things you can do even if you don't have a CD to hand out - yet. You can just offer a report, add them to your newsletter or blog or even offer them a complimentary membership to myAgent TV! Just book a meeting over coffee or lunch and have a strategy session on how you can help them increase the number of quality listings they have, how they can sell them faster for top dollar, and get more control over the quality of their transactions, etc.

That's a good place to start. My point is you need to have a next step after your event to move the relationship forward. Just make sure that you give them a chance to raise their hand and say, "yes, I'm ready for that next step" by following-up and using the tools we've provided for you in this book and at our websites.

Calling No's and Maybe's

You still want to call those no's and maybe's and say, "Hey Mr. / Mrs. Agent, listen, you attended our event and I just wanted to follow-up to see how you liked it?"

"It was great. I loved it."

"Well, I'm just curious. It says on the form, 'If your current lender is not delivering the level of value you'd like, would you be open to talking to us about a possible relationship?' and you put no/maybe. I'm just curious why."

Shut-up and let them talk

"Well, because my wife is my lender," or "You know what, it was a great seminar, but my lender really does a fantastic job and I can't see any reason why I would leave them right now."

"That's fine, no problem. Listen, would you mind if I just keep you on our list of upcoming events and maybe stay in touch periodically, because you never know. Things can change, right?"

"Right. Sure, no problem."

Now you've just gotten permission from what you thought was a, "no, I don't want to talk to you," to market to that agent and a potential future relationship.

That's a maybe which beats a no any day!

I've had originators tell me, "Oh, the agent said they didn't want to meet with me and they're not interested, but I made the thank you follow-up call and they said, 'Hey, you know what, I was thinking about something....'"

"Just the fact that you called really says a lot. Nobody else ever calls to say thank you. Yeah, I'd like to get together with you for coffee."

It's kind of a thank you call, but then it converts into a strategy session or face-to-face meeting of some kind. That's the desired objective, to convert to some face-to-face meetings, right?

PART TWO

The New Rules

The first part of this book introduces you to and explains the *Instant Referrals*™ Seminar System for quickly boosting your agent partners and referrals using educational seminars. Here, Part Two offers you a roadmap to navigate marketing in the Internet Age. You'll soon be effectively elevating yourself from any competition, building instant credibility and becoming the obvious choice for anyone seeking a home loan.

"The future is something which everyone reaches at the rate of 60 minutes an hour, whatever he does, whoever he is."

– C.S. Lewis

Chapter 8

The New Rules of Mortgage Sales & Marketing Success

Have you noticed that marketing has experienced a transformation in recent years? How we reach our target market, get our message out and convert sales has forever changed.

Before the web, Google and Social Media came along; there were only three ways to get noticed: buy expensive advertising or leads, hire a PR firm or bribe mainstream media to tell your story, or hire a huge sales staff and marketing team to cold call people about your products.

That has all changed. Not that we don't want to be calling people, meeting people or not have others telling others about us – we do! The difference today is we have new and more effective options and all are critical to your success. Today the Web allows us to publish relevant content via sites like Facebook, your personal Blog, YouTube etc. and more.

Today we have multiple ways to reach our target market using multiple platforms and media.

WARNING: These new platforms and media are simply tools – nothing more. Like any tool, used incorrectly it can hurt you. Used properly and as part of your overall strategy, these tools can enhance your positioning and infl uence among agents and consumers – but they will *never* replace the power of in person connection and re-lationships.

The New Rules

1) Engage!

As we pointed out in Chapter Three, if you're not *engaged* in your local real estate community – you don't exist. Succeeding with agents requires you to leave your office – actually <u>meeting</u> with agents. Hosting educational (content rich) seminars, is the entry point in your local marketing strategy with agents.

While engaging with agents via Facebook, video and other media is useful, don't fall prey to the bright shiny object syndrome and expect to build a stable of loyal agents referring you their buyers because you posted what you ate for lunch on Facebook or you re-tweeted a bunch of someone else's quotes or because of your automated mortgage rate newsfeed.

One Relationship Is More Valuable Than 1,000 Friends On Facebook

The New Rules of success as a Mortgage Loan Officer today require a blend of both fundamentals and new media. Rely solely on digital engagement with your local agents and your results will stagnate. Rely on automated engagement without context and the human touch and you'll be discovered as inauthentic.

Succeeding today as a Mortgage Professional demands that you position yourself as a leading authority; **IN YOUR LOCAL COM-MUNITY** with.....wait for it...wait for it...*people!*

The fundamentals haven't changed in 200 years. It's relationships that facilitate sales – even more so today.

Unless you originate loans outside your local community, your Social Media strategy for agents and buyers must be *locally* focused.

We've moved from push marketing to pull marketing. The rules have changed. Your success is not based on a particular platform like Facebook or Twitter. Your success as a Mortgage Professional is based on human connection and relationships. Social Media is simply a tool that allows us to reach engage using online media, reaching more people – often in real time.

2) Content Rules!

You've no doubt heard the phrase; "content is king." My friend Gary Vaynerchuck; author of Jab, Jab, Jab Right Hook! says;

"Content is king but marketing is queen and the queen runs the household!"

Me and Gary Vaynerchuck

Your job as a Mortgage Professional is to get homebuyers to engage your services for home loans and referral partners (agents) to send you their homebuyers.

That's what content marketing is all about! Today you have to establish your credibility and authority through educational marketing, success stories, case studies, thought leadership and more. When you deliver relevant content you become a trusted resource.

Be A Problem Solver!

Essentially, good content is anything which solves a problem and/or entertains that is either self-produced or compiled, produced by someone you invite or pay to produce for you. Seminars for your local agents are an ideal method for establishing yourself as a Trusted Authority because of the personal engagement. You should also integrate online to build on the momentum from your live seminars.

Some Examples of Online Content

* Blog posts

* Coupons (Fees, Appraisals, etc)

* Videos

* Audio

* Pictures/Graphics

* Webinars

* Ebooks/Reports/Case Studies

Three Types of Content

* Self-produced

* Other People's

* Conversational

A good integrated content marketing strategy should incorporate the other two additional content marketing strategies; producing (or paying/inviting someone to produce) original content and sharing other people's content.

Sharing other people's content is important to do because it allows you to associate your brand with theirs while building relationships with those whom you are sharing content with.

3) Build Your Opt-In List

Have you noticed that Facebook, Google and others are always changing their rules about how you communicate with your followers?

Let me tell you a story of a friend of mine who did a bang up job, building a following of over 20,000 agents on Facebook. It was a nationwide buyer/seller referral network that mistakenly and innocently used the word REALTOR® in its Facebook Page name.

Well, the word REALTOR® in any form is a registered trademark, owned by the National Association (NAR) of REALTORS®. Much to his surprise, the NAR requested Facebook shut his page down as it was in violation of trademark rules.

Virtually overnight, this thriving community of over 20,000 agents whose names and contact information were exclusively on Facebook, was shut down.

Woosh! That's the sound all that hard work and money as it vanished into thin air with the push of a button.

SPEED TIP

Unless you own the data, you own nothing. You must have a process for building your own, opt-in email list; **referral partners and consumers alike.**

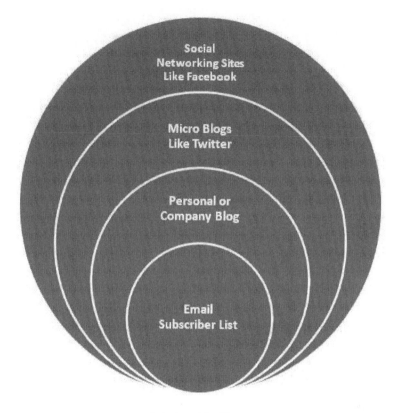

Relationship Rings

The image above shows the various levels of engagement called Relationship Rings. The outer most rings are Social Media sites like Facebook, Twitter, getting more personal with Blogs and and ultimately reaching the most personal level; your email subscriber list.

Remember, you don't want to live on an island. Not if your goal is to engage and connect or to humanize your business. You want to integrate a multimedia strategy for engaging and being a leading authority. Build trust; provide value through good content and your followers will opt in, allowing you to send them relevant emails.

Warning: Abuse the relationship with SPAM, irrelevant content, excessive sales pitches and they'll shut you off – with just a mouse click and you'll have to struggle to rebuild that trust – if you can.

Content Is Not Enough

What? Having consistent, relevant, problem solving content is a key component of your ability to attract referral partners and clients. **But it's not enough!**

Building a competitive edge on content alone is not sustainable. Why? Because today, content is ubiquitous and often overwhelming and people can get pretty much the same content from multiple sources today. Is that a little scary? If it's not about the content and information, what **IS** it about? It's about the authentic connection and relationship that you build with your community and the people in it. When you have that relationship, it's very difficult for anyone else to get their attention, or to attract them away from you.

The Currency of The New Economy

So the secret is to focus on the *relationship* you build with your community so that they TRUST you (which is a key lacking element in the world today). Your content is your entry point in your marketing funnel where people can get to know you, build a connection and cultivate a relationship of value and trust over time.

Provide great content yes! But don't place content over relationship – or you'll lose.

"Whatever you vividly imagine, ardently desire, sincerely believe and enthusiastically act upon must inevitably come to pass."

– Paul J. Meyer

Chapter 9

Success With Social Media

If you're not using Social Media at some level, you are – as we pointed out in Chapter 3 on the Marketing Spiral – not "in the game."

By now I hope you're recognize that no technology, however 'social' it's intended to be will **ever** replace the power of shaking someone's hand and looking them right in the eye, having a meaningful, human connection.

That's the power of seminars you cannot replace with any other tool. In fact, that's what Social Media allows us to do in ways we couldn't do before – connect with other humans!

Technology and the tools will always be changing but human nature remains the same. We want to *connect* with other humans!

Social Media Snake Oil

Have you seen some of the hype with Social Media being touted as the "magic pill" that sends customers stampeding to you and instantly dropping buckets of cash at your feet?

I'm not lambasting Social Media, simply attempting to identify what Social Media really is at its core and how you can best utilize it in an integrated marketing campaign to connect with referral partners and clients.

Social Media marketing by itself without integration into your overall marketing plan will not produce significant results – and will fail over the long term. Relying solely on Social Media for capturing agents, generating buyer referrals and converting leads to customers will leave you disappointed.

Conversation vs. Converting

Social media at its core is a distribution channel for content which allows people to have conversations around and share content.

Most of the content going around on Facebook and Twitter is conversational. There's nothing wrong with conversation which is part of relationship building, but in order to **move from conversation to conversion**, it's not enough.

As a rule of thumb, Twitter Marketing for Dummies author, Kyle Lacy, recommends keeping conversational activity to one third of your Twitter activity.

Sharing Content

Content is the fuel of social interaction on the Web: Nearly one-quarter (23%) of all social media messages and one-half (47%) of industry-specific social messages contain links to content, according to a new study by AOL and Nielsen published May 2011.*

Other key study findings:

Email is the primary content-sharing tool among surveyed consumers (66%), followed social media (28%) and instant messaging (4%).

Most People Share via Multiple Platforms

Nearly all (99%) people who share content via social media also use email to share content.

Some 40% of social media sharers also use email, instant messaging, and message boards to share content.

Formats of Shared Content

Digital content is shared in primarily two ways:

1. **Link-back media: 60% of content shared on social platforms includes a link (URL) to published content on an external site.**

2. **Pass-along media: 36% of content shared on social platforms is embedded.**

3. **Link-back non-media: 4% of content shared includes a link (URL) to a brand or corporate website.**

The study reveals that people share and consume content through multiple mediums. Email marketing is not dead! To reach and engage maximum people, you must leverage all relevant distribution channels – including the most effective – in person!

Make sense?

Ok, so now you're convinced to expand your use of Social Media beyond just posting to Facebook and Twitter but into multiple channels of sharing content – including in person - yes?

In Chapter 4 we learned how to integrate Facebook into your seminar promotion strategy, leveraging your following to get butts in your seminar seats.

*About the study: Findings are based on Nielsen's NM Incite Social Media Monitoring tools, Online Behavior Panel and Attitudinal analysis, tracking more than 10,000 social media messages; and on a survey of more than 1,000 Nielsen Online panel members for 10 consecutive days, December 14-23, 2010.

"Quality is more important than quantity. One home run is much better than two doubles."

– Steve Jobs

Chapter 10

Online Video: The Next Best Thing To Being There

We know online video is hot, but just how hot? Cisco, the company that makes all the routers that power the Internet reports that internet video now accounts for 40% of consumer web traffic, and by the end of 2015, **internet video will be 90%of global consumer internet traffic and 64% of mobile traffic**. That's a huge wave coming at you fast. You can either set your sails to catch the coming wave or have it pass you by.

To succeed with video marketing you must ask yourself; "why would your target market want to watch this?" Most of the time it comes down to these two reasons:

1) To be entertained
2) To be educated

The videos you create will hit on one of those two or ideally both if you can do it.

Who's Watching What?

According to a recent survey commissioned by video ad company YuMe, 49% of people are watching videos daily for an average total of seven hours per week per person.

Seven hours is a lot when you realize that 70% of what people are watching is short form videos less than five minutes long. For long form, TV still rules but the tide is shifting. The majority of the people surveyed said they appreciated the ability to watch web videos whenever they wanted.

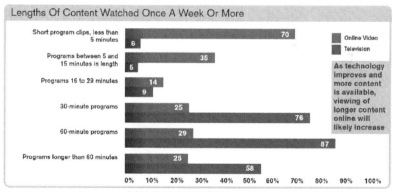

Short-Form Reigns

While the consumption of online video across all content categories is strong, short-form content is the dominant length of content watched regularly online. Specifically, as noted above, 70% of respondents across YuMe's video ad network watch program clips that are shorter than 5 minutes in length, while only 25% watch 30-minute programs and 29% watch 60-minute programs online.

The length of content watched online will inevitably increase as relevant content grows and more people migrate to smart phones, tablets and other devices which make viewing video online easy.

YuMe's biggest takeaway is that the online video consumption is growing and quickly. More than 66% of viewers surveyed said they were watching more video than they did last year. The biggest increase is in women (70% over 30% of men) and the 35-54 age groups (78% over 22% for 18-34). Those numbers prove that the rise in online video usage isn't generational.

Download the YuMe study at our blog: www.LoanOfficerMarketingTV.com under the Resources Tab.

Getting Started With Video

Integrating video into your sales and marketing funnel doesn't have to be a big leap. Here are three ways to use video to stand out from the crowd, create connection and provide value to your referral partners and customers.

1) <u>Showcase Yourself</u> – Consumers are always curious about seeing the people behind a business. Video staff profiles help your employees come to life and can give customers more of a personal connection to you. You could have your Processor, Underwriter and Funder each record a brief video overview of their role in the transaction. Now your consumers have a personal connection, understand more about the loan process and have their questions answered by a real person.

2) <u>Answer Common Questions</u> – Consumers and agents have regular questions that they routinely ask. A sort video or topic focused series may be a quick way to help those customers out. It also might help to reduce the strain on your customer service team by offering online videos of frequent questions. It's a video F.A.Q.

3) <u>Use a Video Survey or Poll</u> - Customer polls and surveys aren't new, but video surveys are. When requesting feedback from customers, consider adding a personal touch by sending the request for feedback with a personal invitation video. You're more likely to get an insightful response with a personal video request. You can even use videos to capture success stories from your happy clients to build out your marketing arsenal and social proof.

Your Own WebTV Show?

Yes, you can! With a webcam, Smartphone or simple camcorder, anyone can do a video web show. It's easier than ever to create video content and share it with your audience.

Record your weekly tips, news and content, edit your video, taking out the flubs and errors using something like (STUDIO) for Windows or iMovie for MAC. Upload your video to YouTube, grab the embed code (easy) and insert into your blog or website, and share the video with your Social Media followers and email subscribers.

You now have your own WebTV show and you'll get better all the time. Online video is only going to get more popular, so you might as well get on board – or you'll likely be washed up on the shore like old driftwood.

SPEED TIP

You don't have to become Steven Spielberg or produce hours of video content that's exclusively yours. You can save time, build credibility and beef-up your content by sharing content others have created along with your own.

In Chapter 6 we introduced you to Top AgentTV. Imagine… your very own personally branded, content sharing platform where agents must go through you to get access to online videos, top agent interviews', marketing downloads, webinars, Social Media training and more.

Imagine your agents watching weekly video tips from top agents and trainers, listening to podcasts of other agents sharing their marketing 'secrets' and giving your agents access to a growing library of tools and resources to help them be more successful in today's market.

You're instantly a top notch content provider adding value and earning trust with your agents.

Learn More at www.TopAgentTV.com

"At its core, a fully functioning business is basically a set of systems and processes."

– John Jantsch; Duct Tape Marketing

Chapter 11

What Business Are You Really In?

So what business are you really in?

I would submit that you are not just a Mortgage Loan Officer or Mortgage Broker/Banker. Hopefully this book has inspired you to recognize that the New Rules force you to become more.

The alternative is to allow yourself to become a commodity and all commodities are reduced to being evaluated by one metric: price.

In the New Rules of Mortgage Marketing it's "survival of the fittest." The *real* business you must be in is the **marketing** and **systems** business that drives and cultivates **relationships.**

Pain of Disconnect

In today's New Economy unless people develop a profound personal preference for you and your company, you'll always struggle to grow your business. As we discussed in Chapter 8, you have to be positioned so that your client or prospect feels like they know you, and that they have a relationship with you so that they literally are choosing you because they **know, like** and **trust** you.

Another way to sustain your partners and clients personal preference for you and your company is to determine how you can create "pain of disconnect" when someone is considering not to continue as your referral partner or client.

Here are a couple of examples:

Once you join Facebook, it's almost impossible to leave because you abandon your entire "life history" and cannot take it with you. I don't know one person over the age of 16 who isn't on Facebook today, and those who have tried to leave seem to always quietly slink back on, realizing the pain of disconnect is too significant.

Apple has massive pain of disconnect if you try and go back to PCs. Most people won't bother trying, but their incredible smart design and entire branding causes you feel disconnected from the feelings of the Apple brand when you consider switching.

Pain of disconnect can mean the emotional feeling they get when dealing with you. It could be about how they feel important or recognized by you. It could be that your service or offering helps solves a major problem for them, and they fear losing out or not being able to solve their problem without you.

Ultimately, if it's painless and easy for your clients to go else-where, don't be surprised when they do. You need to invest in creating services and offerings that your partners and clients "can't live without" that add value to their life and business!

Accidental Success

If you look around your fellow Mortgage Originators you will see people trying to achieve success mostly by repeating accidents. By random acts of marketing, erratic results, yo-yo income etc.

To finally escape this you must have a reliable, predictable, sys-tem that affordably and efficiently delivers abundant quantities of quality prospects and clients.

This book is, of course, rich in examples of Mortgage Origina-tors achieving results with a seminar system for real estate agents, off ering exclusive content to agents via Top AgentTV and more. You've seen the numbers proving that agents are your most quali-fi ed source and method for reaching buyers in today's market.

In order to win the attention, referrals and loyalty of agents you must have a compelling message and "irresistible offer" with pain of disconnect; typically that means content and resources which help agents solve their problems and achieve their goals – along with a solid relationship!

You must build trust with agents to receive their loyalty and have a means of follow-up, nurturing and converting them to referral partners.

Rome wasn't built in a day and although you may be tempted to think this all sounds too complicated or like too much work; this IS the path to freedom from yo-yo income, erratic results, excessive manual labor, cold prospecting and uncertainty in your business.

If you're serious about eliminating the common frustrations most Mortgage Originators face when attempting to succeed with agents, you'll agree that you'll get to work on implementing the systems and processes for attracting, capturing, converting and sustaining agents to profitable referral partners and clients to life-time fans and advocates.

In our final chapter we'll look at the most important key to all your success. Are you ready?

Do you want to know who you are? Don't ask.
Act! Action will delineate and define you.

– Thomas Jefferson

Chapter 12

Let Us March!

There were two great orators from ancient Mediterranean: Demosthenes the Greek and Cicero the Roman. It was said that when Cicero spoke, people exclaimed, "Great speech, wonderful message, we agree." And they showered him with accolades, adoration and standing ovations.

It was said that when Demosthenes spoke, people shouted, "Let Us March!"

Do you notice the difference?

Two great orators; People admired and loved the one. People were gripped and compelled to <u>act</u> by the other.

My hope is this book has provided both the logical and emotional elements needed to inspire you to march forth and conquer! The good news is you are not alone in your quest. We have additional tools and resources to help you succeed!

So let's you and I keep the dialogue going. This isn't goodbye; it's an invitation to connect further.

Our conversation continues online:

Get weekly marketing tips, free tools and more:

The Blog: www.LoanOfficerMarketingTV.com

Follow me on Twitter: @LoanOfficerTV

Join Us @ Facebook.com/LoanOfficerMarketingTV

Before you go, I'd like to say "thank you" for purchasing my book. So a big thanks for choosing this book and reading all the way to the end. Now I'd like ask for a *small* favor.

Could you please take a minute and leave a review for this book on Amazon?

This feedback will help me continue to provide the right kind of infortmation that help you get results. And if you loved it, then please let me know :-)

Contat met direct: gzimpfer@gmail.com / 949-584-9943

If you're up for it, we'd love to profile your success as part of our ongoing series with our community of mortgage professionals. Share your latest video, seminar results or latest win by dropping us a note on Twitter or Facebook.

Checklist For Putting On Wow! Factor Agent Seminars

Call all executive officers of all boards involved in the area and let them know about your plans to hold a very exclusive seminar in the county. Ask for their participation and feedback on date, location, and marketing techniques. The marketing techniques used by many real estate associations to promote a seminar are as follows:

1. Broadcast e-mail/newsletter

2. Voice-Broadcast

3. Board Member magazine/newspaper

4. Board Website/Facebook Page

5. Announcements at all board meetings

6. Advertising placements on flyer racks

Your local board or your Title co-sponsor can provide you a list of all top producers, brokers and managers, in that board. A special promotion campaign can be aimed at those particular people through your company.

Instant Referrals™ Seminar Checklist:

- VIP mailings to Top Agents

- Private lunch with guest speaker

- Direct phone calls and visits from your individual Mortgage Loan Officers (great for business building).

- Direct phone calls and visits from your management (also great for business).

- Solidify a date with a local hotel or other meeting facility.

- Solidify with any guest speaker's the date, time, and subject.

- Prepare marketing materials that include compelling, benefit driven copy for the Real Estate Agents and give to co-sponsors to hand out.

- Think about additional sponsors that would not cause dilution of the primary sponsors and would help defray costs and help promote marketing. Independent Escrow companies, Home Inspection, Staging Services, Termite, Home Warranty, Notary, Homes & Land, Harmon Homes and other related publications.

- Develop a post-mailing/follow-up program to the attendees to convert some of them to referral partners and review their key takeaways of the seminar.

- Check and approve facilities. The date of the seminar should be confirmed with the facility managers. Furthermore, the facility should easily handle the expected number of attendees figuring at least a 30% no-show rate. The facility should have plenty of parking, be air conditioned, and have audio-visual abilities that allow the attendees to see an overhead projector or screen for laptop and Power Point. It would great to have a house audio system or music playing from your laptop before and after the seminar and during any breaks.

- Prepare for a last minute telemarketing blitz, reminding everyone of the seminar and asking everyone to recommit their attendance and remind them to bring their assistant and/or colleague to the seminar.

- Design your presence at the seminar. A table or booth and/or handouts including items that differentiate your company and marketing collateral are appropriate.

- I've also found that anything you giveaway during the seminar creates a lot of excitement and boosts your chances of inducing reciprocation among your audience. (Create a report or free giveaways, CD's, gift certificates, membership to myAgent TV, etc.)

- Obtain lists of managers and other major decision makers that you can either personally call, or send-off a pre-event Voice Broadcast to that will go a long way in developing whole office attendance.

- Have a morning of the seminar meeting with all Mortgage Loan Officers and co-sponsors involved so that the goals of the day can be reinforced.

APPENDIX A

Photo Gallery From Our "LIVE" WOW!! Factor Events

Geoff,

Thanks so much for putting together a terrific event. You made my job easy and packed the room full with 234 agents eager to learn. I would recommend anyone seeking more quality and quantity from their events use your Instant Referrals™ System to fill the room. It sure was a very successful event from my perspective, our co-sponsors and especially the agents.

Les Hewitt
Founder and President
The Power of Focus, Inc.

Event Sponsors

AmeriSpec Home Inspection

Homestead Escrow

APPENDIX B
Sample Event Flyer

Walter Sanford Seminar Flyer

Sample Event Flyer

Mike LaFido Seminar Flyer

APPENDIX C
Instant Referrals Rolodex

I Broker Agent Speakers Bureau (BASB)
Looking for a top notch speaker for your next seminar? My friend
Darlene Lyons has assembled some of the highest quality, Real
Estate and Mortgage speakers in the country.
www.BrokerAgentSpeakersBureau.com

II Call Capture Providers – There are many providers offering
call-capture services. I've compared the fees, services, plans, bells
and whistles of all of them and have provided the following as
the best from my research.

AdTrakker
www.AdTrakker.net
Phone: 800-397-1969

ArchTelecom:
www.ArchTelecom.com
Phone: 800-890-7575

III Reservation Services – There's only one call center service
provider I've used in the past to handle live reservations and
confirmations for my seminars. They take the calls, read your
script, create the list and make one follow-up call to the list prior
to the event.
www.Teledirect.com
Phone: 800-776-1081
*Use Code: Speed to receive 10% off their fees

IV Online Event RSVP – EventBrite is an excellent online platform to handle your online event registrations, list building, name badges, reminders and event website.
www.EventBrite.com

V Real Estate Agent Lists – The most current and accurate list of agents available by zip code, local board, city, state, company with options for email, fax and other data.

VI Zircon Data
www.RealEstateAgentLists.com

VII XL Technologies
Want to send flyers online to your local agents about listings, special programs and events? You can load your own PDF flyer, custom HTML or have them build a flyer for you an email it to agents by zip code and county.
www.eCampaignPro.com

About The Author

Geoff Zimpfer has been helping Mortgage Professionals become the "Go-To" lender in their local area for over 8 years.

His experience as a National Marketing Director and promoter for authors and speakers including Peak Performance Coach Anthony Robbins, Best-selling Author; Brian Tracy, Les Brown, Jim Rohn and America's #1 REALTOR® Walter Sanford, give him unique insights and a successful track record of creating seminars, webinars, videos and marketing campaigns of all kinds that attract new clients, build relationships and increase sales.

An Industry Insider's Perspective

Geoff knows first hand the challenges originators face in capturing business from agents because as a retail Mortgage Originator, his personal loan volume reached $37Million after just three short years – 78% being purchase business referred by real estate agents.

Today, Geoff is helping Mortgage Originators leverage the power and speed of seminars, video, Social Media and other marketing tools to reach top producing agents, break into closed offices, boost origination's, and build deeper client relationships.

As both a husband and father of two active boys, Geoff and his family enjoy the outdoor life in Orange County, California.

Contact Geoff Here: gzimpfer@gmail.com 949-584-9943

Made in the USA
San Bernardino, CA
16 December 2016